A Vindication of En[g...] with Regard to the C[...]

Charles Reginald Haines

Alpha Editions

This edition published in 2024

ISBN : 9789362925329

Design and Setting By
Alpha Editions
www.alphaedis.com
Email - info@alphaedis.com

As per information held with us this book is in Public Domain.
This book is a reproduction of an important historical work. Alpha Editions uses the best technology to reproduce historical work in the same manner it was first published to preserve its original nature. Any marks or number seen are left intentionally to preserve its true form.

Contents

AUTHOR'S PREFACE..- 1 -
A VINDICATION OF ENGLAND'S POLICY WITH
REGARD TO THE OPIUM TRADE....................................- 2 -
Footnotes:..- 49 -

AUTHOR'S PREFACE.

About two years ago I had occasion to go thoroughly into the question of the opium-trade between India and China. Up to that time, knowing practically nothing about the matter except what the Anti-Opium Society and their supporters had to say on the subject, I was as zealous an opponent of the traffic as any of them could wish. But as soon as I came to read both sides of the question, and consult original authorities, I felt myself forced, much against my will at first, to abandon my previous opinions. And I may as well say at once that I have no personal interest whatever, direct or indirect, in the maintenance or defence of the traffic. My only wish has been to treat the[Pg iv] question on the broad principles of practical justice, and not in deference to that cosmopolitan patriotism which would have us love our neighbour not indeed as ourselves, but much more than ourselves. The object therefore of this little work is to clear the fair name of England from the foul aspersions cast upon it by a comparatively small body of well-meaning but misguided philanthropists.

C. R. HAINES.

DOVER, *June 16, 1884.*

A VINDICATION OF ENGLAND'S POLICY WITH REGARD TO THE OPIUM TRADE.

Again there has been a debate in Parliament on the opium traffic:[1] again has the same weary series of platitudes and misrepresentations been repeated, and no one has taken the trouble to defend the policy of England as it should and can be defended. But it is high time that the falsities and the fallacies of the statements of the Anti-opium Society should be exposed, and that everyone to the best of his ability should enlighten the people of England on a subject which so nearly concerns the honour of our country. Isolated voices have indeed been raised to protest against the views disseminated by the Society for the Abolition of the Opium Trade; but these efforts have been too few and far between to reach the mass of the nation. At present the agitators have it all their own way. The majority of people, having heard nothing but what the agitators have told them, denounce the iniquitous traffic with a fervour that varies proportionately with their ignorance. In contemplating the success of this misdirected enthusiasm we are irresistibly reminded of a very "judicious" remark of Hooker's, who says: "Because such as openly reprove supposed disorders of State are taken for principal friends to the common benefit of all, and for men that carry singular freedom of mind; under this fair and plausible colour whatsoever they utter passeth for good and current."

For more than forty years the opium trade between India and China has been a subject for keen discussion and hostile comment in England. Being as it was the *immediate* cause of our first war with China in 1840, the opium traffic could not fail, in Parliament and elsewhere, to be brought prominently before the notice of the people of England, and of course there were not wanting public men to denounce the policy pursued by this country towards China in that matter. This denunciation, at first of a vague and desultory character, took a definite shape in the memorial presented to Her Majesty's Government in the Earl of Shaftesbury's name, and backed by all his great personal authority. The specific charges contained in this document will be noticed hereafter, when we come to sketch the present position of the "Society." Suffice it here to say that it teemed with misstatements and exaggerations of the grossest and most palpable kind, which, having been exposed and refuted again and again, need not detain us now. But so far were those random statements from furthering the cause which the memorialists had at heart, that they only served to steel the minds of unprejudiced people against further representations, however just, from the same quarter.

Since then, however, the agitation has taken a more organized form, and there is now a society for the suppression of the trade, numbering its hundreds of supporters, and linked with the names of such men as Lord

Shaftesbury, Cardinal Manning, Sir J. W. Pease, and Sir Wilfrid Lawson. Nearly the whole of the clergy from the Archbishops downwards, and ministers of every denomination, have declared for the same side. Add to this that the Society has a large income, derived from voluntary subscriptions, which is assiduously employed in the dissemination of its peculiar doctrines. The country is flooded with tracts, pamphlets, reports of addresses, speeches, and petitions, all inculcating the same extreme opinions.

Under these conditions it is not surprising that the anti-opiumists have succeeded in enlisting popular sympathy to a certain extent on their side. But, with the single exception of missionaries, they have against them the vast majority of those who, from personal knowledge and experience, are competent to form an opinion on the subject. Sir Rutherford Alcock, for twenty years Her Majesty's Minister in China, who has had opportunities for forming a correct judgment on the subject such as have fallen to the lot of few, and who can have no bias[2] or prejudice in the matter, has recently before the Society of Arts, in a paper of singular ability and fairness, vindicated the policy of the British Government. Mr. Brereton, for fifteen years resident in Hongkong, has challenged and, on the authority of his own experience, denied *every* assertion of the Anti-opiumists. As to the missionaries, from whom the majority of the arguments against the trade are drawn, no one doubts their good faith, and everyone gives them credit for the best of motives; but, for reasons to be afterwards given, their evidence is likely to be biassed, and in any case cannot be considered worthy to be set against that of all the other residents in China.

But what are the enormities of which England has been guilty? Here is the indictment, stated with all the energy of conviction: That England, and England only, is responsible for the introduction into China of a highly deleterious, if not wholly poisonous, drug, for which, till India took upon herself to supply it, there was in China no demand whatever; that she is responsible, further, for forcing this opium *vi et armis* upon the Chinese, contrary to all obligations of international morality, and in the face of the sincere and determined opposition of the Chinese people; that, in fine, Christian England, with a single eye to gain, is wilfully and deliberately compassing the ruin of heathen China. Such is the indictment brought against England by her own sons; and the tribunal which they would arraign her before is the public opinion of their own countrymen and of Europe.

The original habitat of the poppy plant, which is now extensively cultivated in Asia Minor, Persia, Egypt, India, China, and even in Africa, was probably Central Asia. It must have made its way very early into India, as it is mentioned in the *Laws of Manu*. But it was not till the tenth century that the Hindoos learnt from the Mohammedans the narcotic qualities of the plant.

In China there can be no doubt that opium has been known from the *earliest*[3] times; even if the poppy be not indigenous to that country, as we might be led to suppose from its mention in a Chinese[4] herbal compiled more than two centuries ago. In the *General History of South Yünnan*, published in 1736, opium is noted as a common product of Yung-chang-foo; and it is remarked by Mr. Hobson, Commissioner of Customs at Hankow,[5] that, "if 134 years ago so much opium was produced as to deserve notice in such a work, the production could have been no novelty to the Chinese population at the beginning of the present century, when we began to import it in small quantities." Moreover, it is well known that the seeds of the poppy have been used from time immemorial in the preparation of cakes and confections. Two Court officials were even appointed specially to superintend the making of these for the Emperors' use.[6] Dr. Edkins, in a recent pamphlet on the subject of opium-smoking in China, quotes an edict against the habit published as early as A.D. 1728, and consequently some forty years before the British took any part in the trade. Dr. Wells Williams is of opinion that opium may have been introduced into China from Assam, where it has been used time out of mind. However that may be, the Chinese may be credited with having improved upon their use of it by smoking instead of swallowing it; though this, too, is attributed to the Assamese by Don Sinibaldo de Mas, Spanish Consul in China.[7]

It may, then, be taken for granted that opium-smoking was known to the Chinese long before European nations took to importing opium into China. But at the same time no one will deny that the habit has become enormously more prevalent than it used to be.

The foreign trade in opium is of comparatively recent growth. The Portuguese were the first European nation to import it into China. For some years previous to 1767 they imported from Goa some 200 chests of Turkey opium to Macao. This they would scarcely have done had there been no demand for the drug. It was not till 1773 that the East India Company appeared upon the scene as exporters of opium in very small quantities. In that year the Company assumed the monopoly of the opium culture in India, and, according to the existing Mongol practice, farmed it out for an annual payment in advance. In 1781 a cargo of 1,600 chests was found unsaleable, and re-exported. By 1790, however, the importation into China amounted to 4,054 chests yearly, at which number it remained nearly stationary for thirty years. It was in 1793 first that the ships engaged in the traffic began to be molested, chiefly by pirates, but partly also through the hostility of the Chinese officials. One ship was then sent to Whampoa, an island twelve miles from Canton, where she lay for fifteen months entirely unmolested.

In 1796, however, the first year of Keaking's reign, the importation of opium was prohibited by the Government at Pekin, under heavy penalties, for the alleged reason "that it wasted the time and property of the people of the Inner Land, leading them to exchange their silver and commodities for the vile dirt of the foreigner."

Up to this time, though opium was being imported for the space of more than forty years, not a word had been said against it, and now, when exception *was* taken to it, it was on the ground of the worthless, not the poisonous, nature of the drug, for which so much sycee silver was bartered. This law, like sumptuary laws in general, proved wholly inoperative as far as the Chinese were concerned. The East India Company, however, did so far regard it as to forbid their own ships from engaging in the trade, and their mandate was obeyed. Nevertheless, the trade went on in private ships, and from Whampoa, the headquarters of the trade, the smuggling (if what went on under the very eyes of the custom-house officials can be called smuggling) continued uninterruptedly along the coast, being carried on openly and in the light of day. For though the Government might fulminate against it from Pekin, the officials on the spot, by their undisguised connivance,[8] caused the trade to be established on something like a regular footing. Under which conditions the trade continued for the next twenty years or so with little variation.

In 1816 the Bengal drug first began to suffer from competition with Malwa and Turkey opium, the latter brought from Madeira in American as well as British ships. In 1821 the exportation of Bengal opium had sunk to 2,320 chests, when the Chinese commenced vigorous proceedings against smugglers, and drove the contraband trade to Lintin, an island forty miles from Canton.[9] This seems to have given a fresh impetus to the trade, for the export rose at once to 6,428 chests, and by 1831 to more than 20,000: at which number it remained till Lin's raid in 1839, when 20,291 chests were delivered up and destroyed in the Canton waters.

This violent action of Lin was the outcome of the ascendancy[10] of the Protective party in China; for there can be no doubt that even in Conservative China there was at this time a reform party, headed by the young and accomplished Empress, who advocated enlarged intercourse with foreign states, and, as a step towards this, a less protective policy in trade, including a legalization of the importation of opium. A memorial was even drawn up and presented to the Emperor by Heu Naetze, Vice-President of the Sacrificial Board, in 1829, advocating the legalization of opium. But even the influence of the Empress could not prevail against the prejudices of the Court, and the memorials of Choo Tsun[11] and Heu Kew, who, like Cleon of old, argued for the dignity of the Empire and the danger of instability in maintaining the laws, carried the day. It is not quite clear what grounds of objection to the traffic were held by the Chinese Government, but the *moral* ground, now made so much of, was certainly not one. Between 1836 and

1839 several Imperial edicts were published prohibiting the importation of opium, in which "there is little if any reference to the evils of opium, but very clear language as to the export of bullion."[12] This drain of silver was no doubt the great reason for the Chinese hostility to the traffic. As late as 1829 the balance of trade had been in favour of China, and silver had accumulated; but this state of things had now been reversed, and the increased export of silver—for opium was a very expensive article and had to be paid for clandestinely in hard silver—had begun to cause a great depreciation of cash,[13] the only copper coin of the realm, and to occasion serious alarm at Pekin. Accordingly the Emperor, in pursuance of several memorials on the subject, forbad the export of sycee, at the same time that he took more energetic measures to put a stop to the traffic which was chiefly responsible for this loss of bullion. In 1836 opium ships were prohibited from entering the inner waters of Kunsing-moon, while all foreign ships were detained at Lintin; and the local revenue officers began to show more vigilance in putting down smuggling. In the following year an edict was published prohibiting the continuance of receiving ships in the outer waters, to which Captain Elliott, our Superintendent of Trade, paid little attention, seeing that the Chinese themselves openly disregarded it; and it is even stated that the trade was carried on by four boats under the Viceroy's flag, which paid regular fees to the custom-house and military stations.[14]

In 1834 the East India Company's monopoly of trade to China came to an end, and the trade was taken up by Her Majesty's Government, who sent out a commission with Lord Napier at its head to apprise the Chinese Government of the change. It had been usual up to this period for all communications to be addressed to the Viceroy of Canton through the thirteen "Hong"[15] merchants, in the form of a humble petition. This Lord Napier naturally refused to do, and the Chinese Viceroy resented what he considered the insolent presumption of the "outside barbarians." He declined to receive the Envoy, and ordered a blockade of all the factories. Lord Napier was forced to surrender at discretion, and was escorted back to Macao by an insulting guard of Chinese soldiers, where he died soon after. After this, though the trade was graciously allowed to proceed in its existing unsatisfactory condition, an open rupture between the two Governments was clearly only a question of time. It was evident that the claims of the Chinese to suzerainty over all outside barbarians could not fail to cause one of two things: either a total cessation of intercourse between them and other nations, or a war which should bring them to their senses. Peaceable means to conciliate the Chinese had been tried more than once and had failed. In 1796 Lord Macartney, and in 1816 Lord Amherst, had been sent on missions to effect a peaceable arrangement with regard to trade. Both attempts failed in their object, but served to show the overweening pretensions of the Chinese and their thorough contempt for foreigners.[16] "In both cases," says Sir Rutherford Alcock, "the British mission was paraded before the Chinese population, *en route* from the coast, as tribute-bearers." Lord Amherst was even subjected to personal indignity and insult for refusing to perform the kotow or prostration before the Emperor. Meanwhile, as the power of the Empress and the reform party declined, edicts against opium followed one another in quick succession, but were completely ineffectual in checking the corruption and connivance of the Canton officials, until Lin was appointed Viceroy of Canton, for the avowed purpose of coercing his countrymen and humiliating the foreigner. It was a congenial task, and accordingly we find that immediately upon his arrival in February 1839 he executed a native smuggler opposite the British factories as a menace to his own people and an insult to the barbarians. Early in the following March he issued an edict marked with the "vermilion pencil," forbidding, in the most uncompromising terms, the long-established traffic. With this was coupled a demand for all the opium in the Canton waters. Captain Elliott, who had arrived from Macao in the midst of this crisis, at first refused compliance with this demand, but was starved out, and, like Lord Napier, compelled to surrender at discretion. Lin's victory was complete, and on the whole he used it well. All the opium, to the amount of 20,290 chests was, in the sight of all, sunk in the muddy waters of the estuary. All foreigners were now graciously permitted to depart in peace. But it was evident that the matter could not rest here; for Elliott had guaranteed compensation from the State to those traders who had voluntarily surrendered their opium (which was otherwise quite beyond Lin's reach) in order to release from durance vile the European residents whom Lin had unjustifiably seized. War was now inevitable; but its formal declaration was preceded by one or two collisions between the Chinese and foreign ships. One encounter in the Bay of Coalloon led to the total destruction of a fleet of Chinese junks by the English frigates *Hyacinth* and *Volage*. This was the first experience the Chinese had of our shot and shell, and it should have warned them of what they might have to expect. But it did not. Lin retaliated by a proclamation, addressed to the Queen of England, giving out that for the future "principals in the opium business would be decapitated and accessaries strangled." War followed, and the Chinese were soon brought to their knees. The terms of peace signed at Nankin were the cession of Hongkong, the opening of the ports Canton, Amoy, Foochowfoo, Ningpo, Shanghae, to trade, with consular officers at each place, and an indemnity of six million dollars as the value of opium seized in 1839. The old exclusive trading with "Hong" merchants was abolished, and a fair and regular tariff of import and export customs and other dues was established at the open ports. In this tariff opium was not even mentioned.[17] The author of the *Opium Question Solved* says: "The negotiators dared not mention it; the Emperor would not legalize the hated source of all his humiliations." So the same system of organized smuggling, only carried on now even more openly than before, went on. This smuggling of opium had been the *immediate*[18] cause of the late war; and it was evident that a cordial understanding between the two nations could not be established while this apple of discord remained in their midst. Yet the English Government was very reluctant even to seem to force opium upon the Chinese against their will. Lord Palmerston's instructions to Admiral and Captain Elliott in 1841 on this matter are very precise. This despatch, indicating as it does our policy in this question both at that time and subsequently with unmistakable clearness, may excusably be quoted here.

"In bringing this matter of the trade," he says, "before the Chinese plenipotentiaries, you will state that the admission of opium is *not* one of *demands* you have been instructed to make upon the Chinese Government, and you will not enter upon it in such a way as to lead the Chinese plenipotentiaries to think that it is the intention of Her Majesty's Government to use any compulsion in regard to this matter. But you will point out that it is scarcely possible that a permanent good understanding can be maintained between the two Governments if the opium trade be allowed to remain upon its present footing. It is evident that no exertions of the Chinese authorities can put down the trade on the Chinese coast. It is equally clear that it is wholly out of the power of the British Government to prevent opium from being carried to China. It would seem, therefore, that much additional stability would be given to the friendly relations between the two countries if the Government of China would make up its mind to legalize the importation of opium upon payment of a duty sufficiently moderate to take away from the smuggler the temptation to introduce the commodity without payment of duty. By this means also it is evident that a considerable increase of revenue might be obtained by the Chinese Government, because the sums which are now paid as bribes to the Custom-house officers, would enter the public coffers in the shape of duty."

In accordance with these instructions, Sir H. Pottinger used every argument to persuade the Chinese Commissioners to have the trade legalized. They, while admitting that the suppression of the trade depended upon the Government of China being able to stop the use of the drug, said that they could not yet approach the throne on the subject; but that the Custom-house officers "would not trouble to inquire whether our ships brought opium or not." They even went so far as to say[19] that "on the subject of opium the British and Chinese Governments should adopt their own rules with reference to their own subjects." Sir H. Pottinger intimated his readiness to prohibit our ships from carrying opium into the inner waters of the empire, but the Chinese, he added, must enforce the prohibition. But this was the difficulty; for what could be expected from our measures while the imperial servants winked at the breach of the imperial edicts. The Commissioner,

Keying, then suggested that the Emperor might consent to the legalization of the traffic if a large revenue[20] were *guaranteed* to him. The answer of the British Commissioner was that the British Government did not wish to foster or encourage the trade, but to place it on a less objectionable footing; and, therefore, that Keying's proposal could not be considered. In commenting on these negotiations, Sir H. Pottinger said that the principal *public* reason (bribery and corruption being the private ones) why the truth was disguised, or said to be disguised, from the Emperor, was the inability of the Chinese to prevent opium from entering the rivers and harbours of the empire, or from being consumed by their subjects. The Chinese Commissioner tried to throw the blame on the British Government, asserting that *they* should enforce the prohibition and prevent their subjects from engaging in the trade, a position tenable on no principle of international obligations.[21] The Chinese, then, were unable to stop the traffic and unwilling to legalize it. The mandarins were driven to all kinds of desperate shifts to cloak their imbecility; and Sir H. Pottinger, in one of his last despatches, says: "The mandarins openly give out that they dare not stop the traffic, else it would lead to the cultivation of the poppy in China to so great an extent as to cause a scarcity of food, if not a famine." A truly surprising reason!

However, the arguments of successive British Commissioners seem to have gradually had their effect, and there were not wanting signs that the Chinese authorities were coming round. They were beginning to see that the only way to arrest the hæmorrhage of silver, so alarming to them, which in fifty-four years had amounted to 12,000 tons, was to legalize the traffic in opium, so that the drug might be exchanged for other commodities, instead of, as now, being paid for clandestinely in sterling silver. As a proof that the Chinese were not now in earnest against the traffic, it may be mentioned that not a single proclamation was issued against it since the negotiations between Keying and the English Envoy began. Moreover, as Sir J. Davis wrote to the Earl of Aberdeen, the Chinese did not wish to abolish the traffic, as the impoverished state of the finances of the country did not admit of the servants of the Government being adequately paid in a legitimate manner. So recognized, indeed, had the traffic become, that legal duties even were often paid in opium.[22] But that the smuggling and piracy caused by opium being technically a contraband article were a "womb of evil," was evident to the Chinese themselves, and also that they might any moment be made the excuse for a raid against the foreign community (and there was even a report that Seu, the Imperial Commissioner, was contemplating this), which could only result in a fresh war. So we find that, in spite of their protestations to the contrary, the Chinese Commissioners did refer the matter to the Emperor several times, and on one occasion a decree legalizing the importation was drawn up by his ministers for the Emperor's approval.

When, however, the imperial pleasure was finally taken, Taou Kwang forbad any further reference to the proposal, saying that he could not "change face." So the matter rested for the present. But the advice pressed upon the Emperor that he should legalize the trade did not come from the British Envoys only; for in the *Pekin Gazette* for January 4th, 1853, there appeared a memorial from a Censor, Wootingpoo, who, while admitting that the complete abolition of opium, if that were only possible, would be far the best, points out in forcible terms that as a help to rendering the national advantages fairly and openly available for all, and to removing differences with the barbarians, no measure can compare with that of levying a duty on opium. Alluding to the mine of wealth which lies unworked by China in the opium trade, he defends the policy of making it contribute to pay the expenses of the State, on the principle that of two evils it is always well to choose the least; and he proceeds to enforce his views by showing the impossibility of preventing indulgence in such tastes, which no doubt, when excessive, is pernicious. His estimate of the consumption was £66,666 daily; and he suggested a duty of 11 per cent., which should bring in a revenue of seven million taels[23] a year, whereby the foundations of England's greatness would be sapped. Further, he adds, the increase of native growth will eventually drive out the foreign drug. But this expression of native opinion was disregarded no less than the friendly counsels of our Envoys, and matters went on in the old underhand way till the outbreak of the second war.

On October 8th, 1856, the Chinese officials, in a war-boat, boarded the lorcha *Arrow* as it lay, flying the English flag, in the Canton river, for the alleged reason that it had on board a pirate who was "wanted" by the Chinese authorities. Of the merits of this question it will not be necessary to speak here. It is enough to say that, in all probability, the Chinese were strictly within their right; but, however that may be, it is quite clear that the dispute had nothing whatever to do with opium. Yeh, a man of similar character with Lin and Seu, was Viceroy of Canton, and he promised satisfaction, but withheld it. Admiral Seymour accordingly proceeded to enforce the British claims, and the second war broke out. Owing to the Indian Mutiny, vigorous proceedings against China were deferred till 1858; but when hostilities were resumed Canton was soon captured, and Yeh made prisoner and banished to India, where he shortly died.

But the trouble was not at an end yet; for as the English and French ambassadors,[24] with an escorting squadron, were on their way to Pekin to ratify the treaty which had been drawn up, they were attacked and repulsed before the Taku forts. This brought about a renewal of the war, and Pekin was taken October 1860, and the Treaty of Tientsin was ratified. Five new ports[25] were opened. A British ambassador was to be established at Pekin and a Chinese ambassador in London. Consuls were to be stationed at all the open ports. Not a word was mentioned about opium in the treaty itself, but, in pursuance of Article 26, an agreement was entered into five months later concerning the tariff regulations, wherein "the Chinese Government admitted opium as a legal article of import, not under constraint, but *of their own free will deliberately.*"[26] To a similar effect is the testimony of Mr. Oliphant, another secretary to the mission, whose evidence on this point will readily be considered conclusive. He affirms that he informed the Chinese Commissioner "that he had received instructions from Lord Elgin[27] not to insist on the insertion of the drug in the tariff, should the Chinese Government wish to omit it." But the Commissioner *declined to omit it*. An increase of duty was then proposed, but this was objected to by the Chinese themselves as affording a temptation to smugglers.

It is clear, then, that no force came into play at all, except it were the force of circumstances, and opium—like all other articles except munitions of war and salt, which remained contraband—was admitted under a fixed tariff. This in the case of opium was fixed at thirty taels per picul (133⅓ lbs.), and it was further agreed that opium should only be sold at the port; that the likin or transit dues should be regulated as the Chinese Government thought fit. The terms of this tariff were to be revisable after the lapse of ten years.

Leaving for a moment the question of the foreign import as thus settled, let us turn to the Chinese policy towards their own native growth. The exact date of the introduction of the culture of the poppy into China is unknown; but there can be little doubt that the cultivation has existed for a considerable period. Edicts and proclamations against the cultivation, some of them published last century, are sufficient evidence of this. Mr. Watters, Consul at Ichang on the upper Yangtze, speaks of opium-smoking as having existed *for centuries* in Western China, where, as we know, Indian opium never finds its way. The policy of the Government with regard to this native growth has all along been of a piece with that pursued towards the foreign import. While prohibited by the Government it has been connived at and sanctioned by the local authorities. The reason of this conflict between the local and imperial authorities is clearly pointed out in the recent Parliamentary paper on opium, where a statement of the Consul at Chefoo is quoted to the effect that "the authorities at Pekin have always been hostile to the cultivation of native opium, on the ground of its interfering with the revenue derived from the import of the foreign drug. On the other hand, the local authorities steadily connive at the growth, both from indolence and from the fact that they find it very lucrative themselves, the growers being able and willing to pay largely for the privilege of evading the prohibitions." Under these circumstances it is not surprising that the sanction of the local officials has in most cases prevailed over the prohibition of the Imperial Court; and it is certain that the cultivation had attained considerable proportions by the middle of the present century, for Wootingpoo, in the memorial quoted above, speaks of "gangs of smugglers of *native* opium, numbering hundreds and even thousands, entering walled cities in the west and setting the local governments at defiance." He would have had the prohibition against the native growth withdrawn, as well as that against the foreign import. He answered the chief objection to the native culture, that it took the place of food crops, by pointing out that the poppy was grown in the winter months, and rice in the summer on the same ground. But his representations were of no effect, and the prohibition continued, and was even enforced by a fresh edict, at the instigation of Sheu-kueo-feû,[28] in 1865. How far this edict was effectual it is impossible to say; certain it is that it was flagrantly set at nought by the highest officials. Li Hung Chang, who has lately taken a high moral tone in his correspondence with the Anti-Opium League, actively busied himself in promoting the cultivation of the poppy in the provinces over which he was appointed, alleging, in a memorial to the throne, the importance of the native growth as a source of revenue and as a check on the importation of foreign opium.[29] A fresh edict prohibiting the cultivation was, however, published in the *Pekin Gazette*, January 29, 1869, in answer to a fresh memorial by the Censor Yu Po Chuan; and to this day this prohibition remains unrepealed but obsolete, like the law against infanticide. The poppy is now grown in every province of the Chinese Empire, but the cultivation is far more extensive in the western than the eastern provinces. The two provinces of Yünnan and Szechuen produce by far the largest portion of the drug. Two-thirds of the available land of those two provinces may be said to be under poppy cultivation. The amount of native opium thus produced may be taken to be at least four times as much as the whole amount imported, and the native growth is even encouraged by the duty levied upon it being 50 per cent. less than that levied upon the foreign drug. Such being the case, it is quite impossible to believe that the authorities were ever unanimous or really earnest in their wish to prohibit either the foreign import or the native growth. While the Emperor denounced the foreign traffic from Pekin, and sent Lin to make an example of offenders, the Governor of Canton dealt in opium, and the Emperor's own son was an opium-smoker. Whilst edict followed edict forbidding the growth of the poppy, the Governor-General of a large province openly fostered the cultivation, and the poppy plant flaunted itself in red and white over the half of China. It is useless to assert, as is so often asserted, that the legalization of the foreign trade tied the hands of the Government with regard to the home production. The native growth was well established long before the legalization was effected, and the admission of Indian opium never affected the western provinces of the Empire. Had the Government been in earnest they could have suppressed the cultivation, just as the Taeping rebels did in 1860 in Yünnan.

But to return to the history of the foreign trade. As was mentioned above, the Chinese Commissioners of their own accord fixed the tariff duty upon opium at thirty taels. But, though bound, as they were by their own act, to admit opium at this rate, as soon as it passed into native hands they had power to tax it as they pleased, and they did not fail to profit by their power, though this likin tax varied considerably at the different ports[30] in accordance with the necessities of the provincial governments. It is difficult to estimate the revenue obtained by China from the foreign opium trade, but it is probably close upon two millions sterling. That the Chinese Government were not satisfied with this amount, compared with the profits gained by India, is quite clear; and we find accordingly that various efforts were made by them, subsequent to 1869, to have the tariff agreed upon in the Treaty of Tientsin revised. But it was not till 1876 that any definite agreement was come to between the two Governments. In September of that year Sir Thomas Wade, Secretary Li, and Prince Kung concluded a convention, by which China opened four new ports[31] and six places of call on the great river, while Sir Thomas Wade agreed to recommend to his own Government, and through it to all the Treaty Powers, the limitation of the area, within which imports should be exempt from likin, to the actual space occupied by the foreign settlements. As the treaty regulations then stood, imports, except opium, after paying their regular import duty, were not liable to likin or transit dues till they reached a certain barrier at some distance inland. Opium could be taxed as soon as it left the importer's hands. But this right, which applied to opium only, had been used by the Chinese against all imports, a clear infraction of treaty which the German Consul, among others, had protested against. But as some doubt existed as to where the first inland barrier really stood, Sir Thomas Wade proposed to make the circuit of the foreign settlement the limit of exemption from duty. But foreseeing that, if the likin Collectorate were banished from the port-areas, opium would evade paying the likin tax, he proposed also to recommend that the likin, as well as the import duty, on opium should be collected by the foreign Inspectorate, and that for this purpose the opium should be bonded in a warehouse or receiving hulk till such time as the importer had paid the import due and the purchaser had paid the likin. He further proposed as a fair likin tax forty taels per picul (though certain that the Chinese did not get more than 30) on all Indian opium, that brought to Hongkong included. Thus the whole duty (import and likin) on opium would be seventy taels a picul, which would yield 6,117,930 taels, or a million more than under the old system. But the Chinese Commissioner, Prince Kung, objected to a uniform duty of forty taels, as too low, and suggested sixty taels a picul, or an adherence to the different rates prevailing in different ports. Sir Thomas Wade, though averse to the higher uniform rate, was willing to consider the other alternative, provided that he were informed of the exact position of the next inland Collectorate, and the amount of rates levied. Further, the Chinese Government must guarantee that no second Collectorate should be established between the port Collectorate and the first of the present inland Collectorates. It was agreed by the Chefoo Convention[32] that this collection of the dues on opium by the foreign customs under these conditions should be tried for five years at Shanghae.

Neither the Indian nor the English Government have raised any serious objection to this convention, and the only reason why it is not ratified yet is that the other Treaty Powers will not join in the Shanghae agreement, unless China consents to abolish likin on goods other than opium. Until these other Powers do give in their adhesion, our arrangements must necessarily be inoperative, as opium will be imported under the flag of Powers not parties to it. Pending the ratification of this convention, Sir Thomas Wade offered to give up the concessions granted by the Chinese, and have the ports recently opened closed again; but this the Chinese would not agree to. There now seems every reason to suppose that the difficulties with the other Powers will be got over, and the Chefoo Convention finally ratified.

Before closing this historical survey, we may record the words of the Chinese Commissioner in 1881 to Sir Thomas Wade, when the latter suggested a yearly diminution of the opium sale, that the Chinese *would* have the drug, and that any serious attempt to check the trade must originate with the people themselves. With this sentiment we shall all agree.

It will be necessary now briefly to describe the nature of opium, and its use among, and effect upon, different races.

As a powerful medicine, then, opium, or its principal ingredient morphia, has been known in all ages of the world to all civilized nations, and it may confidently be stated that in the whole range of the Pharmacopœia there is no remedy so unique in its effects, and so indispensable to the efficiency of the healing art as this "much abused drug." As a febrifuge[33] it is invaluable; and, indeed, till the discovery of quinine, stood alone in that respect; while it is of incalculable service in relieving cholera and dysentery[34], and other diseases incidental to a hot climate. It has also a wonderful power of checking consumption, and mitigating its more distressing symptoms.[35] Its efficacy in this respect, though recently denied by Dr. Shearer, is surely beyond all reasonable doubt.

The three chief alkaloid constituents of opium are morphine, narcotine, thebaine, of which the first is the principle peculiar to the poppy, and gives it its stupefying power. The second, narcotine, which in spite of its name has nothing narcotic in it, is a febrifuge and stimulant like quinine; the third, thebaine, affects the nervous system, and is credited by the Chinese with having certain aphrodisiac qualities. Needless to say, however, it is not as a medicine that the opponents of opium find fault with its use, but as a luxury that ensnares the appetite, and enfeebles the mind and body of its hapless votaries. We shall have occasion to show that in the case of the Chinese at least there is an intimate relation between its use as a luxury and as a medicine.

There are three ways in which opium may be consumed: it may be eaten in the shape of pills, drunk as a solution, or smoked as a highly-concentrated extract. And it may here be remarked at once that opium smoked is a quite different thing from opium swallowed, so that arguments proving the pernicious effects of the latter will not of necessity apply to the former at all; while, on the other hand, arguments tending to show the harmlessness of opium eaten or drunk will *a fortiori* prove the innocuousness of opium smoked. The opponents of opium have disregarded this important distinction. Hence much of their evidence against opium-smoking is wholly irrelevant. Sir George Birdwood,[36] relying on the authority of Sir Robert Christison, and on the knowledge derived from personal experience, asserts that opium-smoking *must* be absolutely harmless, as the active principles contained in opium are not volatazable. Theoretically this may be sound enough, but its practical effect upon Asiatics at least can scarcely be reconciled with this supposition. However this may be, opium-smoking is probably not much worse than tobacco-smoking, and far less injurious than dram-drinking; while opium smoked, whatever be its effect upon the system, certainly has not one-tenth part of the potency of opium swallowed. And it is obvious that this must be so, for, when swallowed, all the various constituents of opium are admitted into, and retained by, the stomach; whereas, when smoked, only the narcotizing agent, which is volatizable, finds its way into the system, and that merely momentarily. No doubt opium smoked produces its effect *sooner* than opium swallowed, for it is brought at once into contact with the blood in the lungs, and thus quickly permeates the whole system. The Chinese are generally credited with being the first people to smoke the drug, and the practice is almost confined to them now.

Before, however, speaking of the introduction and spread of the habit in China, we will briefly notice those countries where some form of opium-consumption is prevalent, and endeavour to point out the general effects observable therefrom. And we are in a position to form a correct judgment in this matter, for there is a considerable consumption of opium in British India, so to speak, under our own eyes. The districts in which this consumption is most prevalent are Rajpootana, parts of the Punjaub, Orissa, Assam, and Burmah. In Rajpootana, among the Sikhs, the drinking of "umal pawnee," a solution of opium, is a common custom extending to women and even children as well as men. They take their glass of laudanum as we take our glass of wine. And though this habit is of long standing, and indulged in by at least 12 per cent. of the inhabitants of the country, no such wholesale ruin and demoralization has been caused as the declamations of the anti-opiumists would lead us to expect.[37] Indeed, the Sikhs are physically the finest race in India,[38] and show as yet no signs of degeneration. Dr. Moore, for some time Superintendent-General of Dispensaries in Rajpootana, assures us that he has known individuals who had consumed opium all their lives, and at forty, fifty, sixty, and even older, were as hale and hearty as any of their fellows. Opium, then, even when swallowed, cannot, as it appears, do the Rajpoots much harm. In some cases it is undoubtedly highly beneficial. "When taken," says Dr. Moore,[39] "by the camel-feeders in the sandy deserts of Western Rajpootana, it is used to enable the men, far away from towns or even from desert villages, to subsist on scanty food, and to bear without injury the excessive cold of the desert winter night, and the scorching rays of the desert sun. When used by the impoverished ryot, it occupies the void resulting from insufficient food or from food deficient in nourishment; and it not only affords the ill-nourished cultivator, unable to procure or store liquor, a taste of that exhilaration of spirits which arises from good wine, but also enables him to undergo his daily fatigue with far less waste of tissue than would otherwise occur. To the 'kossid,' or runner,[40] obliged to travel a long distance, it is invaluable." It may be added that opium *smoking* is almost entirely unknown in Rajpootana.

Passing on to the Punjaub, it appears from the recent report on the Excise in that province, that, though a large part of the rural population have a preference for opium above spirits, a preference derived from custom and religious prejudice; yet they are compelled to take to the latter, and the yet more deleterious "bhang,"[41] owing to a growing disinclination among the cultivators to cultivate opium under such strict Government supervision as is enforced, combined with a diminution in the amount imported. This state of things is deplored by the Excise officers, who recommend an increased importation to meet the demand which undoubtedly exists. In this province opium is smoked to a considerable extent under the name of kossúmba.

In Orissa the consumption of the drug is very general, and has much increased since the famine of 1866. According to Dr. Vincent Richards,[42] who instituted a statistical inquiry for the purpose of eliciting trustworthy information, from 8 to 10 per cent. of the adult population of Balasore take opium, those living in unhealthy localities being much more addicted to it than others. Moderation is the rule, but even excessive doses of the drug are taken without any very serious ill-effects, while its efficacy in cases of fever, elephantiasis, and rheumatism, is undoubted.

In Assam, as might be expected from the unhealthy and malarious character of its soil, opium is freely resorted to, and Assam has been singled out by Dr. Christlieb—one of the most strenuous, and we may add misinformed, supporters of the anti-opium league—as affording the most striking evidence of the disastrous use of opium in India. Among other things that pernicious drug is credited with producing barrenness; a result which, as Dr. Moore has conclusively shown, is due entirely to the unhealthy nature of the soil, and may even be counteracted by a moderate use of opium. Residence in low, swampy districts creates a natural craving for opium, as the statistics of our own islands will abundantly testify. Throughout the British islands, the only districts where the consumption of opium can be said to be at all common are in the fen country of Cambridgeshire, Lincolnshire, and Norfolk.

Lastly, we come to British Burmah; and here undoubtedly the case against opium *seems*, at first sight, overwhelming. But those who have only read what the anti-opiumists have said about it, will have formed a very one-sided notion of the facts of the case. Till 1870 a comparatively small quantity of opium was imported into that country, but in the succeeding decade the amount rose from 15,000 to 46,000 sears.[43] This was apparently owing to the direct encouragement of the Government. The habit of *eating*[44] or smoking opium (for—and this is an important point—both are practised) spread with fearful rapidity even among the population of the villages, especially among the rising generation. The physical and mental deterioration in those who contracted the evil habit, and the consequent increase of misery and crime brought about a strong expression of native feeling against the practice. "To put away the accursed thing entirely was the only advice that appeared to the native elders of any value at all."[45] The Government, as a recent writer in the *Times*[46] says, promptly took advantage of this feeling to close forty out of the sixty-eight opium shops, and raise the price of opium 30 per cent., at a loss to the provincial revenues of from. £50,000 to £70,000. No one will question the wisdom of these measures; but there can be little doubt that on the one hand the demoralization caused by the spread of the vice was exaggerated,[47] while on the other the guilt of the Government is not so flagrantly evident, for there never were more than sixty-eight shops in 87,000 square miles of country. No one could lawfully possess more than one ounce of opium outside a licensed shop, and the law, if broken, was promptly vindicated. "The Government sales, when highest, were only enough to satisfy 3 per cent. of the adult male population."[48]

We are tempted to ask what was the cause of this sudden increase in the consumption of opium. Increased facilities for its purchase was undoubtedly one cause, but Sir Charles Aitchison supplies us with another important one. "The people,"[49] he says, "are becoming emancipated from many restrictions of their old creed. The inevitable tendency of the education we give, and of the new sense of personal liberty which our Government creates among an Oriental people, is to weaken the sanctions of religious belief, and break down the restraints of social customs."[50] So far, and this is all that a perusal of anti-opium publications will tell us, the contention that opium is wholly pernicious seems fully borne out. But, as before pointed out, a proof of the injuriousness of opium-*eating* is no proof that opium-smoking is injurious; and the zealous denouncers of the drug have omitted to mention all in the Report which tells strongly against their own case. At the very beginning of the memorandum the Commissioner says: "The Chinese population in British Burmah, and to some extent also the immigrants from India, especially Chittagonians and Bengalese, habitually consume opium without any apparent ill-effects; those of them who have acquired the habit do not regularly indulge to excess. With the Burmese and other indigenous races the case is different. The Burmese seem quite incapable of using the drug in moderation."[51] So that if there were no other difference between the Chinese and Burmans in their appetite for opium, there would be this, that the one habitually smokes in moderation, the other habitually indulges to excess. Further, one of the arguments brought forward by the Commissioner against the total closing of all shops, a step clamoured for by the anti-opiumists, not to mention the obvious difficulty of preventing smuggling, is that "the *legitimate requirements* of the 200,000 Chinese and natives of Bengal, resident in British Burmah, must be considered and provided for. These, to whom the drug is a *necessary of life*, constitute perhaps the most thriving and industrious section of the population."[52] It will be seen, then, that we cannot argue from the effect of opium on the Burmese to its effect upon the Chinese.

The greater part of the opium consumed in India is supplied from the Government stores under the name of "abkari," or excise opium.[53] Four thousand chests are issued yearly for this purpose from the reserve stock of Bengal opium; but this year it has been decided to allow Malwa opium, for which the market is at present very slack, to supply this. Besides this excise opium, which is never sold at a rate low enough to encourage export, some little opium is imported from the Hill states, and a small quantity is grown in Rajpootana, the Punjaub, and the Central Provinces, under strict Government supervision and for local consumption only.

Besides in India opium is eaten in Turkey, where its virtues are so much appreciated that the legend stamped on the opium lozenges is "Mash-Allah," the "Gift of God"; and the habit is prevalent in Persia also. Among the Malays and Siamese, and in Java and Sumatra and the neighbouring islands, it is mostly smoked; and, of course, the Chinese carry the habit with them wherever they go. Even America has caught the infection, and the rapid progress of the habit, especially among the lower orders, called forth vigorous coercive measures. It may be that these will have the desired effect; but that will only be because the Americans have no natural craving for the drug, and prefer their national taste for gin and whiskey and rum. Some of the more violent opio-phobists, pointing to the spread of this "horrid and infectious vice" among the Americans, hint in almost triumphant tones that the secret use of opium in England is already considerable, and still increasing, as though it were a Nemesis, too long delayed, for her crimes.[54] If we may believe De Quincey,[55] opium-eating was by no means an uncommon thing among the upper classes, even in his day; and Dickens, in his description of an opium-den in *Edwin Drood*, draws no doubt upon his stores of personal knowledge acquired in his youthful rambles among the streets of London. However, we cannot think there is any real danger of the English people deliberately taking to opium. Tobacco answers every purpose. But it is an undoubted fact that the mortality among children in large towns like Bradford and Manchester is due, in a great measure, to their being unwittingly dosed with opium, which enters largely into the composition of soothing syrups, cordials, and elixirs of all kinds.[56] It has been estimated that 300,000 lbs. of opium are imported annually into the United Kingdom, only a part of which can be used medicinally.[57]

Before speaking more particularly of the political agitation against our policy with regard to opium, it will be necessary to state shortly what that policy has been in the case of India. The opium from which India derives her revenue is of two kinds, called respectively Bengal and Malwa opium. The former is that grown by the Government agencies at Patna and Benares; the latter, that grown by the native states of Scindia and Holkar, which has to pay a heavy duty in passing through our territory. With regard to the Government monopoly of Bengal opium, our policy has been very vacillating in past time; and mainly to this cause may be ascribed the fluctuations in the revenue derived from this source. The opium revenue amounted in 1838 to £1,586,445 net, which by 1857 had risen to £5,918,375. In 1871 the large total of £7,657,213 was reached, and this has been still further increased in the last decade to eight and a half millions. The constancy of increase noticeable in the revenue for the last few years has been due in great measure to the adoption of a plan proposed by Sir Cecil Beadon in 1867 that a reserve stock of opium should be formed from the abundance of fruitful years to supply the deficiencies of lean ones; so that a certain fixed amount of the drug might be brought into the market every year. This reserve stock, which amounted in 1878 to 48,500 chests, by constant demands upon it has diminished to 12,000 chests. The amount sold yearly has, in consequence, been lowered from 56,400 to 53,700 chests, and a further reduction to 50,000 chests is contemplated.[58] The revenue, therefore, is not likely to be in excess of the amount received 1881-2, which was eight and a half millions (net), of which three and a half millions are due to the export duty on Malwa, the other five millions to the direct profit on the Bengal drug.

The amount of land at present under opium cultivation in British India is about 500,000 acres,[59] and this amount does not admit of any considerable extension.

It was in 1826 first that the East India Company made an agreement with Holkar and other native chiefs that the former should have the exclusive right to purchase all opium grown in the table-land of Malwa.[60] But, in spite of this agreement, opium grown in these estates found its way to the Portuguese ports of Damaum and Diu on the Persian Gulf, for export to China. Consequently, after an unsuccessful attempt to limit the production in the native states, which almost occasioned a civil war, the existing system was abandoned, and a tax upon opium exported through Bombay substituted.

The number of chests annually exported out of India is about 45,000, which gives the Indian Government a revenue of £3,150,000; whereas a similar amount of Bengal would bring in five and a half millions sterling. It is difficult to estimate the exact revenue that accrues to the native princes from the culture of the poppy, but in any case it must form a main portion of their whole income, amounting in some cases to as much as half, in spite of the enormous duty we can lay upon its export. The cultivation is very popular in the native states, and the people, we may be sure, have no scruple in supplying China or any other nation that will buy their produce. "No rajah," says Dr. Christlieb, "under a purely native system, would administer the opium revenue as we do; the Brahmins would soon starve him out." What this remark precisely means, it is difficult, perhaps impossible, to discover; but the general meaning desired to be conveyed, no doubt, is that a native ruler would not be allowed to engage in so iniquitous a traffic by the superior sense of justice and morality inherent in his Brahmin councillors. Credat Judæus! Whether it would be possible[61] or in accordance with justice, or consistent with the policy hitherto pursued towards the native states, to prevent opium from being grown by the native princes (if so be that the doctrines of the anti-opium league find favour in the sight of Englishmen), is a question which will be more fully dealt with when we come to discuss the remedial measures proposed by the denouncers of our opium policy. We only know that our last attempt at interference in this matter well-nigh caused a civil war.

Allowing, then, for all deductions on the score of "abkari" opium, and for a certain amount which the French colony of Chandernagore have a right to purchase at existing rates, we may say that about 95,000 chests of provision opium are exported from India every year: 45,000 chests of Malwa from

Bombay, and 50,000 of Bengal opium from Calcutta. But it is a mistake to suppose that all this goes directly to China proper. About 1,000 chests a month, or more than one-fifth part of the whole annual amount sold at Calcutta, goes to supply the needs of the Chinese in the Straits Settlements and thereabouts, in Cochin China and Cambogia, and of the Siamese and Malays. Moreover, a considerable quantity is deflected at Hongkong for the use of the Chinese in California[62] and in the Philippine, Fiji, and other islands. The exact amount so deflected it is impossible to estimate;[63] but we may feel pretty sure that not much more than 80,000 chests of Indian opium are sold in China itself. The Bengal opium finds a better sale than the Malwa, partly from its inherent superiority and partly from the Government guarantee being affixed. Its price is very high, being 460 taels per picul or chest,[64] while native opium is only 350 taels, including transit dues.

The use of Indian opium is consequently restricted to the richer classes, and the poorer classes have to put up with the native drug. At present there is little fear that the native drug will drive out Indian opium, as there seems to be some peculiarity of soil or preparation which makes Bengal opium superior to all other kinds.

The present import tariff paid by Indian opium varies at the different ports, but is about thirty taels in most; and this brings in to the Chinese Government (including likin or transit dues),[65] about £2,000,000 a year. This they seek to increase by being allowed to levy a higher duty on the imported article than they themselves suggested after the Treaty of Tientsin. The negotiations on this subject have been already described, so we need not dwell upon them here. The English Government are naturally unwilling to agree to any large increase of duty, such as would afford a temptation to smugglers and restore the former unsatisfactory condition of things, while in all probability just as much Indian opium would find its way into China, the duty being at the same time evaded. But it is a mistake to say that the Chinese are powerless to tax opium, for they can place any transit duty they please upon it as soon as it has left the importer's hands, and they have not failed to avail themselves of this privilege, thereby causing in their own borders much successful smuggling. If the Chinese were allowed to double the import duty on Indian opium as they proposed to Sir Thomas Wade, and if they were able, as they formerly were distinctly unable, to prevent smuggling, our profits on the drug would no doubt be diminished in proportion to the increase of duty, and this rivalry would presumably lead to a compromise. But apart from this contingency there are two ways in which the opium revenue might be lost to India. On the one hand, by natural competition with other kinds of opium the Indian drug might be driven from the field. This, for many reasons, is unlikely. On the other hand, the political agitation against the trade, if successful, would have the effect of putting a sudden and complete stop to the traffic; and it behoves us to consider, in a calm and dispassionate manner, how far such a consummation is desirable, and, if desirable, how far it is practicable.

First, how far is it desirable? And here let us premise, with Major (now Sir Evelyn) Baring,[66] "that facts cannot be altered or their significance attenuated by any enunciation of abstract principles." Violent denunciations from platform and pulpit, combined with a persistent ignoring of the exigencies of the case, as though they were irrelevant matters, are not likely to commend themselves to those responsible ministers, either in England or India, who have to face the financial and political problems connected inseparably with any attempt to abolish the opium trade. It is really no answer to the financial difficulty to say, as the Lord Mayor[67] said at a meeting held at the Mansion House, "that the financial difficulty would be got over if the Government would only deal with the question and do what is right." Nor is it easy to believe that the English taxpayers will come forward with five millions a year as compensation to India. Those who seem to advocate this step do not fail to remind us of the £20,000,000 spent for the emancipation of slaves as a "glorious precedent." But the difference between the two cases need not be pointed out: they must be obvious to all. What the exact remedies proposed by the opponents of the traffic are, it is difficult to define; for, united as is their condemnation of the present policy with regard to the trade, they are by no means as unanimous in suggesting a policy of their own.

The various objections to the trade were first formulated in Lord Shaftesbury's memorial to Lord Clarendon in 1855. The challenge thus thrown down was at once taken up by Sir John Bowring, our Superintendent of Trade in China, who, as might be expected, knew somewhat more about the matter than the enthusiastic memorialists at home. He may be taken to have disproved all the most important allegations contained in that document, namely, that the trade was exclusively British; that the annual death-rate from opium rose to the "appalling" figure of more than a million; that the Chinese were really in earnest about prohibiting the traffic. Some of these points have been abandoned; others are considered irrelevant to the question really at issue, which is held to be whether any interference with the fiscal policy of a foreign state be in itself justifiable—whether, that is, we are warranted in keeping China to her treaty-obligations to admit opium at a certain rate. It is quite natural that they should wish to confine the discussion to this their strongest point, but we are not disposed to allow that this is the real or only point at issue; and we will therefore take the main charges levelled against the opium trade separately, and endeavour to do them full justice.

These are: 1st. Opium is a poison, and *therefore* opium-smoking as practised by the Chinese is poisoning the people. 2nd. We are responsible for the introduction of this habit into China. "We have held the poisoned chalice," an eloquent Bishop has said, "to the lips of the Chinese and forced them to drink it." 3rd. We have even forced it upon them, and are still forcing it. 4th. We hold a monopoly in the manufacture of opium, but a monopoly is always economically wrong, and the monopoly of a poison is morally indefensible. 5. This traffic is an insurmountable barrier to the labours of our missionaries. Let us take them in this order.

1. It is stated that opium in any form is a poison pure and simple, and has been declared to be so by Act of Parliament: that, moreover, its pleasures are so seductive that the habit of taking it, once established, can never be forgone, so that the moderate smoker glides almost imperceptibly, but no less certainly, into the excessive smoker: that this immoderate indulgence impoverishes the fortunes, mars the morality, and ruins the health of the victim himself, and plants the seeds of disease and vice in his children. This count in the indictment will not be quite complete unless we add, on the authority of the missionaries, that opium-smoking is all but universal, and the annual mortality due to it one million at least. As to the latter estimate, we may say with the late Dr. Medhurst, himself a zealous and enlightened medical missionary, that it "has not even the semblance of truth, but is an outrageous exaggeration." What the exact number of deaths from this cause may be is by no means so easy to discover;[68] for, apart from the fact that there is no register of deaths to appeal to, it would be impossible to decide how many even of the deaths caused by opium could be attributed to the habit of smoking opium as a luxury, for many of them, as has been pointed out, might be due to suicide,[69] for self-destruction by opium[70] seems as common a practice with the Chinese as suicide by drowning is with us. But there is another and more fertile element of error; for many, and probably the vast majority of cases so pathetically described by missionaries, of victims[71] to the vice in hospitals and dying by the roadside, are cases of men afflicted with some painful or incurable disorder who have taken to opium-smoking, as De Quincey did to opium-eating, as a relief and a solace. To such, indeed, it is a priceless boon, and it may well be doubted whether it is not oftener the means of prolonging life than of shortening it.[72] Much has been made of the evidence of T. T. Cooper before the Parliamentary Commission in 1871, where he says that he frequently saw men dying by the roadside, *simply from want of opium*. Yet it is difficult to see how he ascertained the cause of death in each case. He seems rather to have jumped at a conclusion, as he certainly did in another part of his evidence, where he gravely affirms that, in his opinion, were the opium supply to be suddenly cut off, *one-third* of the adult population of China would die! Why, to begin with, one-third of the adult population do not even now, after the lapse of ten years, in which the spread of the habit has been unchecked, smoke opium; no, nor any number approaching it. Secondly, it has been proved in the case of prisoners, whose supply of opium is always stopped when they

enter the jail,[73] that a sudden deprivation of the drug does not cause death. Again, opium is held accountable for pauperism, dishonesty, crime, and depravity of all sorts. That indulgence of any kind is a sign of moral weakness, and likely further to deprave the moral nature, is undeniable, but (and here we have Dr. Myers with us) "though excessive opium may hasten the effects of a general moral depravity, we are inclined to think that it is much more often rather a sequence than a cause." "In China," says Mr. Lay, "the spendthrift, the man of lewd habits, the drunkard, and a large assortment of bad characters slide into the opium-smoker: hence the drug seems chargeable with all the vices of the country." There will be no need to point out that opium is not the cause of all the pauperism and vice that exists among the Chinese people; for a vast amount of pauperism is common to all Eastern races, and dishonesty, untruthfulness, cruelty, and vice of the most revolting kind, were characteristic of the Chinese long before opium was so common as it now is.

What, then, are the effects of opium-smoking on the Chinese individually and as a nation? Had they been anything like what the anti-opiumists assert they must be, surely the effect would be visible after all these years in an increased death-rate or a decreased birth-rate. Needless to say, no such aggregate result is observable. Where opium is most smoked, there the population is most thriving and industrious,[74] and increases the fastest. "No China resident," says Dr. Ayres, colonial surgeon at Hongkong, "believes in the terrible frequency of the dull, sodden-witted, debilitated opium-smoker, met with in print." Mr. Gregory, H.M.'s Consul at Swatow, says: "I have *never* seen a single case of opium intoxication, although living with and travelling for months and hundreds of miles with opium-smokers."[75] Dr. Myers, after ten years' medical practice in different parts of China, confesses that his "preconceived prejudices with reference to the universally baneful effects of the drug had been severely shaken." Again, it was estimated by the colonial surgeon at Hongkong, in 1855, that there were more deaths from drunkenness in Hongkong among the 600 Europeans than from opium among the 60,000 Chinamen. Similar testimony is borne by a recent medical report of the Straits Settlements,[76] wherein, under the head "poisons," it appears that there were from alcoholic poisoning thirty-nine deaths, of which twenty-six were Europeans, three Chinese, one Malay, nine Indians; while from opium only five in all—a result all the more significant as there are at least 300,000 Chinese in the Straits Settlements,[77] and only about 4,000 Europeans, including the military. Dr. Hobson, another medical missionary, and as such entirely averse to the trade, says: "Opium-smoking is not nearly so fatal to life as spirit-drinking is with us; its use is even compatible with longevity." It is very common to hear Chinese acknowledge that they have smoked opium for ten, twenty, or thirty years. Dr. Hobson mentions one case in which the smoker began at nineteen, and smoked for fifty-one years.[78] Further evidence is surely unnecessary to prove that opium-smoking is not necessarily, nor even commonly, destructive of life. Even opium-eating, *a far worse vice*, for it "sets up an incessant and cumulative craving, so that a rapid increase of dose is necessary"—not even opium-eating is inevitably fatal, as the case of the Rajpoots proves. De Quincey, as is well known, took 8,000 drops of laudanum a day for some time, which is equivalent to thirty-two grains, and two grains of opium swallowed are equal in effects to fifty-eight grains (one mace) smoked, three mace being a smoker's usual allowance.[79]

Though we cannot state for certain the number of deaths from opium, we can form a rough estimate of the number of smokers supplied by the Indian drug; and this has been done by Mr. Hart, Inspector-General of Chinese Customs. But his figures need some modification, inasmuch as he puts the number of chests imported at 100,000, whereas the number, for reasons given above, certainly does not exceed 85,000 all told. Moreover, he reckons the population of China at 300,000,000—surely a low estimate. We may safely assume it to be 350,000,000. Again, in his estimate of the native drug he errs on the other side, for the amount of the native drug produced is probably much more than 100,000 chests, and may be even four times as much.[80] Mr. Hart's figures, then, thus amended, give the following results:—Indian opium imported to China amounts to 85,000[81] chests at most = 8,500,000 catties (1⅓ lb.). Provision opium, when boiled down and converted into prepared opium, loses at least 30 per cent. of its weight; consequently 8,500,000 catties of provision opium are equivalent to 5,950,000 catties of prepared drug, which = 952,000,000 mace (58 grains). This is sold at 800 taels per 100 catties, so that the whole quantity imported costs 47,600,000 taels, or £14,280,000, the price per mace being a little more than 3½d. English. Average smokers take three mace of prepared opium a day, and spend 11d. Dividing the number of mace smoked by the days in the year, we get 2,608,219 mace as the amount smoked daily, at the cost of £39,123. As the average smoker takes three mace a day, there must be 869,406 smokers of the Indian drug, *i.e.* one person in every 400, or ¼ per cent. The smokers of the native drug may be taken—a large estimate—to be four times as numerous. Still the two together will only form 1¼ per cent. of the population. The native drug costs only half as much as the Indian, so that the whole native crop, being four times as much, will only cost twice as much, or £28,560,000. The whole amount, then, spent by China on native and Indian opium will be £42,840,000 a year, and the number of smokers 4,347,000, of whom India is responsible for 870,000.[82] Not that we are to suppose these 4⅓ millions of smokers to be all indulgers to excess. That is no more the case than that all who drink wine and spirits in this country are habitual drunkards. There is, indeed, in the case of each individual a well-defined limit, of which he knows that so far he can go with safety, and no further. This curious fact we owe to Dr. Myers,[83] who also gives it as his experience that opium-smokers may be divided into two classes:[84] "1st. The minority, who, from being rich, can afford to gratify their tastes. Of these the official class are less prone to excess than those well-to-do persons who suffer from idleness and ennui. 2nd. The majority, consisting of persons who have to work hard for their livings, among whom moderation is the rule." For, that opium does not destroy a capacity for hard physical[85] and intellectual[86] work, nay, even enhances it, has been abundantly proved, and that not only when taken on emergencies, but also when habitually indulged in.

In a recent letter to the *Times*[87] from a correspondent at the Straits Settlements, some interesting facts are recorded with regard to the use of opium there. The Chinese population of the Straits Settlements and the neighbourhood cannot be much more than one million souls. About 12,000 chests of Bengal opium are imported yearly, being more than one-seventh of the total amount of Indian opium exported. It appears, then, that the Chinese of the Straits Settlements, who are the finest specimens[88] of their race in existence, consume one-seventh part of the opium consumed by 175,000,000 Chinese, the other 175,000,000 being held to consume the native drug. Or, if the Straits scale of consumption prevails in China, then the quantity of opium imported is only enough to reach one-fiftieth part of the Chinese population, leaving the remaining forty-nine fiftieths to consume the home-grown article. The correspondent goes on to say: "According to the descriptions circulated by the Anti-Opium Society of decimation, emaciation, &c., the Straits Chinamen ought to be all dead men. But they live to disprove the anti-opium theory. Nay more, they are robust, energetic, and hearty beyond all other Eastern races."

It has, we think, been sufficiently proved that, though opium is strictly a poison, and if you take too much of it you must probably, as De Quincey says, "do what is particularly disagreeable to any man of regular habits, viz. die," yet taken in moderation it is, for the most part, harmless, if not beneficial.

We will now advert to the second charge, and endeavour to point out that we are not responsible for the introduction of opium into China, either as having first brought it to the notice of the Chinese, or as having planted in them a craving for it, which is really due partly to climatic causes, partly to constitutional characteristics.

From the history of the traffic given above, it will abundantly appear that the poppy was known and cultivated in China—to what extent it is impossible to define, but certainly to some extent—*long* before any foreign opium found its way into the empire. But even if this were not so, the English would not be responsible for the first importation of foreign opium, since the Portuguese preceded them by some years. Not that the Portuguese or any other nation can be said to have created a craving for the drug among the Chinese by the mere fact of supplying it, as Mr. Storrs Turner insists, for such a view of the conditions of supply and demand is, we take it, untenable. We may be sure that in those early days, before the haughty Celestial had felt the power of the outside barbarians, whom he thoroughly despised and consistently ill-treated, he would have laughed to scorn the idea that a few foreign traders could force upon him anything he was determined not to have. But the truth is that the Chinese people, *literati*, gentry and all, did ardently covet this foreign drug; and there are surely weighty reasons—if we will only condescend to investigate them—to justify their preference.

Every nation, as has been repeatedly pointed out,[89] whether civilized or barbarous, in all ages of the world, has been addicted to the use of some stimulant or narcotic.[90] Of these there are more than fifty kinds in use in different regions of the globe, ranging from alcohol in Europe, to "pombe," a fermentation from millet, in Africa, and from bhang or hemp in India to coca and tobacco in America. Samshoo, a fiery distillation from rice, is the intoxicant of Japan, and was that of China before opium took its place.[91] The West Indians extract a strong spirit-rum from sugar-cane. Even the Kamschatkans draw an intoxicating liquor from mushrooms; even the Siberians express the juice of the crab-apple for the same purpose.[92] What but the natural craving of mankind for some intoxicant or narcotic "to make glad the heart of man" can have brought about the independent discovery and use of so many stimulants? For what purpose but to satisfy such a craving can Nature have scattered in such profusion the materials for its gratification? It has been said, and all known facts bear out the assertion, that "the craving for such indulgence, and the habit of gratifying it, are little less universal than the desire for, and the practice of, consuming the necessary materials of our common food." Not but that there are gradations in the wholesomeness of these several stimulants. Perhaps the most purely beneficial is coca, which has, in some unexplained way, the power of retarding waste of tissue, and at the same time increasing nerve-power. Next to it in value undoubtedly comes opium, both because it also, to a great extent, has this effect upon the tissues and on the nervous system, and also owing to its curative and sanative powers. Of the three principles of which it consists—morphine, narcotine, thebaine—the first supplies the intoxicating and nerve-affecting element; while the second base, the narcotine, is the tonic and febrifuge which makes the drug so valuable in the treatment of bowel complaints, and as a safeguard against ague and malaria. This naturally brings us to the reasons which have made opium-smoking so prevalent in China. These are, as before stated, partly climatic, partly constitutional. Taking the former first, we may note that China over one-third of its surface is a vast ill-drained marsh, and covered to a large extent with rice-fields, the cultivation of which is productive of much unhealthiness.[93] To counteract this unhealthiness, nothing is so efficacious or so handy as opium; for, though quinine is even more useful as a febrifuge, opium has the additional advantage, peculiar to itself, of checking blood-spitting and consumption, a disease fatally prevalent in these unwholesome localities. As a general rule, the unhealthier the locality is, the more opium is consumed there, not in China only, but in India (*e.g.* in Orissa and Assam), and in our own fen districts. But besides being a safeguard against malaria and its attendant ailments, opium is also a valuable agent in counteracting the effect of the putrid and unwholesome food which, by its piquancy, pleases the Celestial palate. But over and above these special reasons, there are general causes which predispose the Chinese to *some* lazy habit. Their home life is not one which affords them many attractions. They have no books, except the everlasting *Confucius*, and no periodical literature to engage their thoughts. The domestic life of the Chinese has none of the charms implied by our word "home"; and it is this blankness, this want of home attractions, which no doubt causes much of the drunkenness of the poorer classes here in England. The gin-shop is the poor man's club. Lastly, opium is specially suited to the lethargic Turanian nature,[94] for while by the delightful dreamy sensations which it produces it supplies the place of an imagination which the Chinaman lacks, it does not rob him of that dignified repose, that impassive acquiescence, which is so marked a characteristic of the Oriental mind.[95]

And here it will not be amiss to institute a short comparison between the use of opium by the Chinese and the use of ardent spirits by ourselves. Those who agitate for a suppression of the opium trade demur to any such comparison being made; and naturally, for it tells entirely against them.

Dr. Hobson,[96] a member of the London Missionary Society, and for many years medical officer at Canton, says: "I place alcohol (the bane of Great Britain) and opium (the bane of China) in the same category, and on the same level, as to the general injurious influence upon society: what may be said against the latter may be said with equal truth against the former.... Opium is probably more seductive and tenacious than alcohol; and I should certainly affirm that it was not so frequently fatal to life, nor so fruitful of disease and crime, as is the case with intoxicating drinks in Great Britain."

Dr. Eatwell says: "Proofs are still wanting to show that the moderate use of opium produces more pernicious effects than the moderate use of spirituous liquors; while it is certain that the consequences of the abuse of the former are less appalling in their effects upon the victims, and less disastrous to society, than the consequences of the abuse of the latter."

Sir Henry Pottinger says:[97] "I believe that not one-hundredth part of the evils spring from it that arise in England from the use of spirituous liquors."

These witnesses, and they might be indefinitely multiplied, will be enough to show that there is no intrinsic difference between opium and alcohol such as to justify exceptional legislation in the case of the one which is not afforded to the other. What difference there is is wholly to the advantage of opium. We may go further than Dr. Eatwell, and say that there *is* ample evidence to prove that the moderate use of opium—and nine-tenths of those who smoke it use it in moderation—is *not* more injurious than the common use of wine and beer with us. Taken to excess, its effects, even if the worst accounts of its opponents be literally accepted, are no whit worse than, if they can be as bad as, the delirium tremens of the confirmed drunkard. "Physically," says Sirr,[98] "the effect of opium on the enslaved victim is almost beyond the power of language to pourtray." "It is impossible," writes another author, speaking of drink, "to exaggerate—impossible even truthfully to paint—the effects of this evil, either on those who are addicted to it, or on those who suffer from it." It would be easy, were it necessary, to quote descriptions of the visible physical effects of opium and alcohol upon their victims—so much alike that they could with very little verbal and no essential alteration be applied to either indifferently. It will be enough to point out where opium has the decided advantage over alcohol. One point in which this advantage is manifest will be obvious to all, and indeed is conceded by the bitterest opponents of the drug. Alcohol makes men noisy and quarrelsome, and maddens them till they are ready to commit any crime and perpetrate any outrage; opium lulls its votary into a dreamy rest quite incompatible with any violent or passionate action. Our gaols are filled with prisoners who, under the influence of drink, have committed horrible crimes.[99] Indeed, nine-tenths of all our prisoners owe their incarceration to their fatal propensity for drink. Everyone is familiar with the terrible accounts of wives beaten and kicked to death by husbands infuriated with drink. By far the largest proportion of murders of any kind are due to the same cause. Convictions for drunkenness and disorderly conduct number 170,000 every year. Our lunatic asylums owe at least thirty per cent.[100] of their patients to the "stuff that steals away men's brains." Nothing so bad as this has been, or can be, said of opium. But opium has another incalculable advantage over alcohol, for the disorders which it occasions are *functional* only, whereas alcohol causes *organic* disease—a most important difference surely; for once get the opium-smoker or eater to forgo his luxury, though the wrench may be severe at first, he will shortly be restored to *complete* health. This, we need not say, is not the case with the confirmed drunkard. He may, indeed, give up his fatal indulgence; but he has planted the seeds of disease in his body, and no art can eradicate them. His very blood has assimilated the "flowing poison," and the heart is no longer the centre of life, but of death. The dipsomaniac, even if he escape the horrors of a death by delirium tremens, falls a victim to paralysis or heart disease. Happy indeed would it be if our drunkards could be converted into opium-smokers, and the desirability of effecting this has even been pointed out by medical men.[101]

But there is one point in which alcohol is considered very generally to have the distinct advantage over opium. The opponents of the latter say that it is much more seductive in its temptation than alcohol, as well as more tenacious in its grip; in fact, they roundly assert that while the use of alcohol *can* be forgone, even by a confirmed dipsomaniac, opium grows more and more necessary the longer it is indulged in, and can only be resigned with life itself. Facts seem to have no force with these champions of a theory, or we might remind them that the Emperor Taou Kwang was himself a slave to the habit, but emancipated himself, as many others have done, among them our own De Quincey, for whom the task was so much the harder inasmuch as he drank the poison to the extent, for some time, of 8,000 drops of laudanum a day.[102] A Chinaman, writing to the *Times* in 1875, says: "I have not yet seen or heard of a case where a confirmed opium-smoker could not reform himself if he had been compelled to leave off his vicious habit by necessity or from determined resolution." So much for the tenacity of the habit; but we are not disposed to admit even that it is more seductive than alcohol, for have we not Dr. Myers' opinion that "his experience both in Formosa and in other parts of China would go to support the statement that the use of opium through the medium of the pipe does not, at least up to a certain point, irresistibly and inherently tend to provoke excess, as is very often the case with the stimulants indulged in by foreigners."

Sufficient evidence has been produced to show that alcohol is productive of far more evil than opium, inasmuch as the former, though beneficial to most people when taken in moderation, yet with others acts as a virulent poison, even in the smallest quantities; while taken in excess its immediate effect is to make the drunkard like a "beast with lower pleasures," to bring out, in fact, the lower side of our nature, and to incite to deeds of violence and crime; and its certain subsequent result is disease, madness, and death. Opium, however, like alcohol, when taken in moderation is a comfort and a solace to thousands, and, while soothing and relieving the body, acts[103] in such a way on the brain as to quicken the intellectual faculties, and not in the manner of alcohol to deaden them. The opposite effects of opium and alcohol, the one in quickening,[104] the other in deadening the faculties, may be gathered from the fact that the Chinese indulge in the pipe *before* entering upon business matters, while we reserve our wine till the matter in hand has been fully discussed. At the same time it may be admitted that excessive indulgence in opium impairs the fortune and health, and, like every other self-indulgence, weakens the moral nature of the victims to its "bewitching influence." This being so, the unprejudiced observer will ask with wonder why those who are so indignant about the opium traffic, do not turn their attention with the same zeal to the suppression of the traffic in spirits at home. The Chinese Emperor was reported to have said, and the sentiment has been extolled to the skies by the anti-opiumists: "I will not consent to derive a revenue from the misery and vice of my people." The English people, however, are not so fastidious, and our annual revenue from the duty on spirituous liquors is £27,000,000, and on tobacco £8,500,000, while our partiality to alcohol costs us £145,000,000. The Chinese, with a population ten times as great, only spend £42,000,000 on their luxury, opium, and derive a revenue therefrom, in spite of the Emperor's disclaimer, of more than three millions sterling. India exports to China about 5,300 tons of crude opium, which together with four times the amount of native-grown drug gives 2½ oz. (avoird.) to each individual. We in England, with a population of thirty-three millions, consume 200,000 tons of alcohol, not to mention more than a billion gallons of wine and beer.[105] And the annual mortality resulting from this terrible indulgence in spirituous liquors is 128,000, while the number of habitual drunkards is 600,000;[106] that is, one in every 260 persons dies from over-indulgence in alcohol! What an appaling fact! we might say, echoing Lord Shaftesbury's words. Terrible as it is, it has been accepted by our countrymen as a deplorable necessity which cannot be altered by any legislative enactments against the importation of alcoholic drinks from abroad. All, or all except a few visionary enthusiasts, have come to see that the only way to check this widespread vice is by bringing the opinion of the people to bear upon it, to drive it out from among the lower classes as it has been driven out from the upper by the force of public example and public opinion. It is obvious that the same reasoning will apply to China[107], and accordingly we find that the drinking of samshoo, a deletrious extract from rice, was common among the people, and all prohibitions were powerless to prevent it till the religious influence of Buddhism was brought to bear upon it and had great success in diminishing the vice; so that samshoo-drinking is now comparatively rare in a great part of China, its place being taken by opium, which is allowed by Buddhist and Mohammedan laws.

But, say the anti-opiumists, if we have not introduced opium into China, we have certainly forced it upon the Chinese when they showed a sincere desire to have none of it; first by a system of armed smuggling; secondly, by open armed intervention in the wars of 1840 and 1857; and thirdly, by the imperious logic of Lord Elgin and others. Now, as to the armed smugglers, the answer is easy. They were armed to resist pirates, who swarm in the bays and creeks so abundant in the Chinese coast-line of 3,500 miles; and by no means, as implied, to fall foul of the Custom House officials. These were always amenable enough, and a recognized bribe paid in due time freed all opium vessels from farther molestation in that quarter. The second assumption, that the wars were opium wars, false as it is in reality when thus stated, is a most plausible one; for opium was certainly the *immediate* cause of the first war. But it was not the real cause. European ideas of the equality of nations could not be reconciled with the insolent pretensions of the Chinese with regard to all foreigners. This, and much more to the same effect, has already been dwelt upon in the historical survey, and so need not detain us any longer now. We may, however, add that no mention whatever of opium was made in the Nankin Treaty, so that the edicts against the drug remained in force, though they were no more regarded now than before the war. And this was certainly not because the Chinese were exhausted by the war and afraid of a fresh conflict with the English. It is doubtful whether the authorities at Pekin really considered themselves beaten at all, and the reason why their edicts were disregarded was not that defeat had weakened the hands of the executive, but, as before, simply the corruption of the officials, and the imperious desire of the people for the drug. With regard to the second war, it is absurd to call that an opium war. Opium had nothing to do with its commencement, renewal, or end; nor was it even alluded to in the Treaty of Tientsin. It was only some months after the ratification of that treaty that in arranging the tariff of imports the Chinese Commissioner himself suggested that opium should pay a fixed tariff and be admitted as a legal import. No doubt Lord Elgin, and here he was seconded by the American Minister, as Sir Henry Pottinger and Sir J. Davis before the war, pointed out to the Chinese how eminently desirable it was that this "stone of offence" should be removed, but in reality it was the persuasive logic of facts which induced the Chinese to propose the legalization of the import. This second war, like the former one, was undertaken by the English[108] to exact compensation for injury to British subjects, and to make the Chinese understand that foreign nations were entitled to, and would exact fair and respectful usage. The French waged war to avenge the murder of a missionary, M. Chapdelaine, in 1856, so that we may in strict justice call this a missionary war; and certainly that part of the Treaty of Tientsin which may be said to have been wrung from the Chinese most against their wills is that which gives missionaries—Protestant as well as Roman Catholic—an entrance into any part of China, and extends to them while there, and to their converts, the protection of their respective Governments.[109]

So far, then, the evidence as to force breaks down entirely, but it cannot be denied that in a certain sense the Chinese are coerced in respect of the tariff on opium. This was fixed in the convention following the Treaty of Tientsin, with the condition attached that the tariff could be revised after ten years. And the Chinese have expressed a desire to alter the tariff by raising the dues on opium. The negotiations between Sir Thomas Wade and Prince Kung have been given at length above,[110] so it will only be necessary here to repeat that the Home Government have not seen their way yet to accept Sir Thomas' proposal;[111] and consequently (and here lies the one strong plea of the anti-opiumists) as the matter now stands, the Chinese are prevented from raising the import duty on opium, though they can alter the likin as much as they please. This may be fully conceded. What would be the result of allowing China free liberty in this matter will be discussed hereafter; but we may be allowed to remark here, that in this hasty denunciation of force applied to China, the eloquent advocates for the suppression of the opium trade forget that we are guilty of forcing not only opium and missionaries, but ourselves as a nation, our commerce, our civilization in their entirety, on an unwilling and exclusive people. On the abstract justice of such a course we need not dwell. It is enough to say that it has been pursued by the stronger towards the weaker in all ages of the world, and no treaty has ever been imposed upon an Asiatic by an European Power except by force.

The next objection refers to our *monopoly* of the drug, some finding fault with it as economically wrong, others as morally indefensible. To the former, who like Sir Charles Trevelyan and Sir William Muir wish to substitute a "pass" system for the monopoly, it may be answered, as it has been answered before and always with success, that monopolies are a part of the system of Indian Government inherited from their Mohammedan predecessors; and any argument against the opium monopoly applies with tenfold force to the salt tax. Moreover, the Indian Government, it must be remembered, is the great landowner in India, and consequently the only undertaker of great enterprises, such as irrigation works and railways. Still it cannot be denied that, technically, the objection is sound enough, because monopolies tend to restrict labour and capital, and entail considerable cost in the production of the article monopolized. But it must not be forgotten that "in direct proportion to the removal of the economic objections, the moral objections would be intensified in degree."[112] For if the Government abandoned the manufacture of opium to private enterprise, contenting itself with placing a duty on its export, there can be no doubt that more opium would be manufactured and imported into China, while the revenue would be less. Moreover, if it be wrong to grow opium for Chinese consumption we shall not get out of the responsibility of it by placing a duty on all opium exported instead of growing and selling it ourselves.

Lastly, there is the objection that our introduction of opium into China paralyses the efforts of our missionaries. We have reserved this charge till the last, both because it has done more than any other with certain classes of people to bring discredit on the traffic, and also because it has been least adequately met by other writers on the subject. And the question is a very delicate one to discuss. It may seem presumptuous to call in question a statement of fact lying so entirely within the scope of a missionary's observation; and it certainly will seem invidious to point out, as we shall be obliged to do, the real causes of failure in our missionary efforts, presuming them to have failed.

Our missionaries, then, almost unanimously assert that "opium has been the means of closing millions of Chinese hearts to the influence of Christian preaching," partly by setting the Chinese against foreigners in general and Englishmen in particular, but chiefly by supplying them with a ready-made argument against the Christian religion as one that tolerates so iniquitous a traffic to the ruin of a friendly nation. Dr. Medhurst[113] supplies us with a sufficient answer to this. "If we do supply the opium, why do you smoke it? Why do you even grow it?" But, in truth, whatever ingenious arguments the astute Chinaman may use to justify his rejection of the new doctrine, the reason of the ill success of our missionaries is not to be found here. For why, if opium be the only obstacle to conversion, are we not more successful in India? There are in the whole of British India only 900,000 converted Christians, of whom far the largest number are Roman Catholic "hereditary" Christians, about a quarter of a million being Protestants of various denominations. "Of course there are some," says a correspondent to the *Times*, "perhaps even a considerable number, whose views of life are really elevated by their Christianity; but it is a fact worthy of all attention that really devout Indians who have, under the influence of Christian teaching, cast off Hindooism, have preferred to create a new and, as they say, a purer religion for themselves, rather than accept Christianity in the form in which it is presented to them by the missionaries." The "Brama Somaj" is indeed worthy of all consideration, but obviously cannot be discussed here. Missionaries in India impute their failure to the advantages given by Government to secular education. The Japanese again,[114] though their orators confess that they are no bigoted adherents of any creed, that their minds are like blank paper, fitted to receive new characters from the pen of any ready writer, decline to embrace Christianity because they do not consider it a good religion; for they see that it does not prevent the English from being licentious and brutal to their coolies, and from having no reverence for old age. Such excuses, and they are mere excuses, are fatally easy; and while Christian practice differs so much from Christian profession, will always remain a weapon of offence against the followers of Christ in the hands of unbelievers. But so far from opium being a barrier to the acceptance of the Christian religion, it has been the means[115] indirectly of opening the gate of the empire for the admission of Western ideas, and, among them, for the introduction of the Gospel of Christ.

"The passion of the Chinese for opium," says one writer, "was the first link in the chain which was destined to connect them at some future day with all the other families of mankind." Again, it may reasonably be asked with Sir

John Bowring, "whether the greater proportionate number of native professing Christians is not to be found in those districts where opium is most consumed, and how the undoubted fact is to be explained that in Siam, where the Siamese do not smoke the drug, there is scarcely a solitary instance of conversion among the native population, while among the Chinese and other foreign settlers in Siam who habitually employ it, conversions are many." What, then, are the causes of our failure? Dr. Hobson, himself a medical missionary, and by no means an apologist for the traffic, says, "Our chief obstacle at Canton is the unfriendly character of the people." And there can be no doubt that this inveterate hostility exists all over China against foreigners in general and missionaries in particular, and has repeatedly shown itself in outbreaks of brutal violence against foreign residents, culminating in the murder of M. Chapdelaine in 1856, and the massacre of the French Mission together with the Consul and several Russian residents at Tientsin in 1870. Later still, we have had the murder of Mr. Margary in Yünnan. This hatred is intensified in the case of missionaries by their civil[116] and political action, and by the fact of Roman Catholic Governments exterritorializing all their converts, *i.e.* making them for all intents and purposes their own subjects, and releasing them from all subjection to Chinese authority. This establishment of an "*imperium in imperio*" cannot fail to be intolerable to an independent State, even if it be consistent with the idea of a State at all. Moreover, the admission of missionaries no less than of opium is a permanent badge of their defeat in several wars, and the sense of humiliation aggravates their dislike for the "outer barbarians." So that we can believe Prince Kung's wish, expressed to Sir Rutherford Alcock, to have been a heart-felt one: "Take away," he said, "your opium and your missionaries, and we need have no more trouble in China." Of the two, indeed, they hate missionaries most, for did not their most powerful mandarins, Li Hung Chang[117] and Tso Tsung Taang, say to Sir Thomas Wade, "*Of the two evils we would prefer to have your opium, if you will take away all your missionaries.*" Sir Rutherford Alcock gave similar evidence before the Commission in 1871: "The Chinese," he said, "if at liberty to do so, would exterminate every missionary and their converts."[118] But cordially as they detest all missionaries, who, backed by their respective Governments,[119] assume a protectorate over their converts, their bitterest hate is reserved for the Romanists. These penetrate into the interior, and aggregate property, own land, and houses, and pagodas, and are now some of the largest landed proprietors in the different localities. They have even gained the right, by the French Treaty, of reclaiming whatever lands and houses belonged to the Christian communities when the persecution and expulsion of the Jesuits took place in the seventeenth century. But besides the hostility of the *literati* and gentry, other causes are at work to render the labours of our missionaries abortive. Chief among these is one mentioned in a publication by the Church

Missionary Society itself, called the *Story of the Fuh-kien Mission*. "Christianity," says Mr. Wolfe, a missionary at Foochow, "would be tolerated too, and the Chinese would be easily induced to accept Christ among the number of their gods, if it could be content with the same terms on which all the other systems are willing to be received, viz. that no one of them claims to be absolute and exclusive truth. Now, as Christianity does claim this, and openly avows its determination to expel by moral force every rival system from the altars of this nation, it naturally at first appears strange and presumptuous to this people."[120] Very similar in old times was the attitude of the Roman polytheism towards the various religions with which it was brought into contact. It was tolerant of all religions and non-religions except (*a*) exclusive and aggressive ones, like Christianity and Judaism; (*b*) national ones, like Druidism; and (*c*) extravagant and mystic ones, like the worship of Isis. So now the Buddhists and Taouists would be ready enough to associate the religion of Christ with that of Buddha or Laoutze, seeing indeed, as they say, little difference between the doctrines of Buddha and of Christ.

Buddhism was introduced into China at the very time when in the West the Fall of Jerusalem had set Christianity free from its dependence on Judaism, and enabled it to go forth in its own might, conquering and to conquer, till it became the religion of the whole Roman world. The name of Christ was not heard in China till 600 years later; and it was not till 1575 A.D. that a permanent Jesuit mission was established in that distant land. This being the case, it is not to be wondered at that the Chinese are unwilling to renounce a religion in many respects as pure and as moral a one as the pagan world has ever seen, and one which they have held for eighteen centuries, in favour of a creed, as it would seem to them, of yesterday, and one which the hated foreigner seeks to force upon them at the point of the bayonet; for the war of 1857 *was* a missionary war, though not by any means an opium war; and it is only by the Treaty of Tientsin that missionaries have any right to preach Christianity in China. Previously to this Christianity had been forbidden by King Yoong-t-ching in 1723, and that edict had never been repealed.

But though these two causes, the hostility of the people and the assumed intellectual superiority of the Buddhists and Confucianists, render the path of our missionaries unusually difficult, and fully account for their ill success, yet it may be asked why the Roman Catholic missionaries are more successful than ours. Both the above reasons apply to them as strongly, or even more strongly, than to Protestant missionaries. They have even an additional disadvantage in their confessional with women, a proceeding which is looked upon with the greatest suspicion by the Chinese who, as far as possible, seclude their women from the sight of all men. Perhaps, as has been hinted at by a correspondent to the *Times*, the celibacy of the Roman Catholic priesthood, an institution which they hold in common with the priests of

Buddha, impresses the people with a favourable view of the religion. But there are other reasons.

As mentioned already, the Jesuits established themselves in China at the latter part of the sixteenth century. They first landed at Ningpo, and thence made their way to Pekin,[121] where, "by good policy, scientific acquirements, and conciliatory demeanour, they won the good-will of the people and the toleration of the Government." In 1692, Kang Hi published an edict permitting the propagation of Christianity. From the success of these Jesuits, sanguine expectations were entertained in Europe of the speedy evangelization of China—hopes that were not destined to be realized. Various causes conspired to effect their downfall in China, principally connected with the political state of Europe at that time. In 1723 Christianity was prohibited, and the Jesuits expelled. "The extinction of the Order of Jesuits," says Sir George Staunton, in the preface to his *Penal Code of China*, "caused the adoption of a plan of conversion more *strict*, and probably more orthodox, but, in the same proportion, more unaccommodating to the prejudices of the people, and more alarming to the jealousies of the Government. Generally speaking, it threw the profession *into less able hands*, and the cause of Christianity and of Europe lost much of its lustre and influence. The Jesuits were generally *artists* and men of science, as well as religious teachers." There can be no doubt that this was the main secret of their success; and in order to ensure like success, we must send out missionaries of like stamp, men of high genius and refined education, who have grasped the theory of Aryan civilization; who can meet the Buddhist, and the Hindoo, and the Confucianist on their own ground; who, going forth in the spirit of Our Lord's words, "I come not to destroy, but to fulfil," can, if necessary, graft the law of Christ on the doctrines of Buddha. Let them treat Vishnoo and Buddha as St. Paul treated Venus and Mars, and say to a people given up to idolatry, "Whom ye ignorantly worship, Him declare we unto you." Not that we would counsel them to make any sacrifice of principle in order to secure converts, as the Romanists seem to have done; such a course must be fatal: and, indeed, "these unworthy concessions to the habits of vice and superstition so prevalent in China" have already been a serious obstacle to the spread of the true doctrine;[122] for enquirers have expressed their readiness to join the Church if, like the people belonging to the religion of the "Lord of Heaven" (*i.e.* Romanism), they may continue opium-smoking, and work as usual upon the Lord's Day. So successful in one sense have these tactics been, that the Roman Catholic missionaries claim to have 30,000 converts in the province of Fuh-kien alone, mostly hereditary Christians of the fifth generation. These so-called Christians are, however, very ignorant of Scripture, and in most respects indistinguishable from heathens. For instance, they identify the Virgin Mary with one of their deities called Seng Mu, or Holy Mother, and pay idolatrous worship to her. Such success need not be envied by our missionaries.

The two points, then, in which the Roman Catholic missions have had the advantage over Protestant ones are—1st. Their missionaries, especially the earlier ones, were far more able men than the generality of our mission clergy. "You may get men," says a writer to the *Times*,[123] "of average attainments to go abroad as missionaries, just as you get clerks and engineers. But they who adopt propagandism as a means of living—and it is no disparagement to the missionaries that they do so—are not exactly the men to impart a living impulse to the hearts of masses of people. Xaviers and Bishop Pattesons, indeed, appear at intervals to prove that the apostolic spirit is not yet extinct among men; but such exceptional phenomena fail to redeem the commonplace character of the ordinary missionary field-force." 2nd. The Roman Catholic faith, by its very oneness, by its remarkable similarity to the institutions of Buddhism, and by its concessions to some of the grosser instincts of the human mind, no less than by having a united and organized Church behind it, cannot fail to commend itself more readily to the minds of the heathen than the more spiritual and independent, but at the same time more narrow and sectarian, beliefs which are all ranked as branches of the Reformed Church. "Thinking[124] they are invading a country as soldiers of the Cross, these young missionaries go forth, denouncing the beliefs, the traditions, the worship of the people, calling on them to curse all that they have ever held sacred, and to accept, on pain of eternal perdition, the peculiar arrangements of beliefs which the missionary has compounded for them, and of which Christianity is one, but not always a very perceptible ingredient; and so the poor heathen, hungering, however unconsciously, for the bread of life, is offered instead the shibboleths of a very Babel of sects." But though they have failed as yet in the higher aim which they have set before themselves, the efforts of the missionaries have been wonderfully successful, though they care not for this success, in raising the social standard of the people with whom they are brought into contact. "They deserve infinite praise for the way they have created written languages where none existed, and for their assiduity in educating and civilizing thousands of savages."[125]

Our missionaries, then, who deserve every credit for their noble and self-sacrificing efforts in the cause of Christ, who in the face of difficulties such as few can appreciate, do their Master's work with cheerfulness and zeal, in spite of danger and privation, comparing their own failure with the success of missionaries elsewhere, as, for instance, in Madagascar, and seeking to account for it before their countrymen at home, miss the true causes which we have been compelled, however ungraciously, to point out, and, taking the nominal objection from the mouths of their opponents, with heedless confidence assert that opium is the great obstacle to the propagation of the

Gospel, forgetting that it was the difficulties connected with opium that first opened a way for them into the heart of China; that it was the second opium war, as they love to call it, which gave them a *locus standi* in the country. But, in truth, in comparing their work with that of their fellow-workers in Africa and elsewhere, they are placing themselves at an enormous disadvantage; for we must not forget that in China and India we are dealing with races[126] immeasurably superior to the North American Indians and the savages of Africa; that we are confronted by civilizations which were in their prime when England was inhabited by naked savages, and was indeed, as the Chinese still believe it to be, but as "an anthill in the ocean," and by a race of men who were "learned," as Cobden said in the House of Commons, "when our Plantagenet kings could not write, and who had a system of logic before Aristotle, and a code of morals before Socrates." It would be surprising indeed if we could persuade such intellectual and civilised races to give up in a moment beliefs which have taken centuries to mature; and the difficulty is the greater in the case of the Buddhists from the striking similarity which exists between the general principles professed by followers of Buddha and disciples of Christ. "Conversion to Christianity," as Dr. Moore says, "involves the belief in certain statements the counterparts of which, when found in Buddhism, are regarded as impossible and untrue by Christians."

What, then, should a missionary do in the face of all these difficulties? Let him follow Dr. Medhurst's advice, and remember that "the effectual fervent prayer of a righteous man availeth much"; let him exhort the Chinese to abandon the habit of opium-smoking, and compel their converts to give up the drug; and, above all, let him be careful not to make exaggerated statements about the opium traffic, which merely tend to disquiet the minds of his countrymen at home, and, when the falsity of his statements becomes apparent, to throw discredit on the cause which he has at heart. But if the missionary's duty is clear, no less clearly is it *our* duty who remain at home to make the most strenuous efforts to aid the good cause by subscribing more largely to the missionary fund (instead of expending our money for the purpose of raising an agitation against opium in England), and so, by increasing the remuneration offered to workers in this large field (for the labourer is worthy of his hire), to induce the ablest and most intellectual of our clergy to go out to encounter Buddhism and Taouism—opponents quite worthy of our steel—feeling sure that success, though delayed, is certain in the end, and that the Chinese only need to become Christians in order to be one of the greatest nations upon earth.

It remains now only to mention the remedies proposed by the supporters of the Anti-Opium Society for the evils of the opium traffic, pointing out such objections as may occur to us; and finally to state the alternative course which we ourselves propose. We may premise, however, before dealing with this part of the subject, that there is a considerable divergence of opinion manifest in the ranks of the Anti-Opium Society with regard to the nature of the remedies suggested. Some are for merely washing our hands of the monopoly, so that the Government would have no direct participation in the *manufacture* of the drug, but would, by means of an export duty, retain more or less of the revenue therefrom. This course, it must be said, does not find favour with the majority, who demand, consistently enough, the total abandonment by India of the manufacture of opium *and* the revenue from it.

Let us consider the less radical proposal first.

As long ago as 1832, the question of abolishing the opium monopoly suggested itself to the East India Company; and the same course was proposed by Sir Charles Trevelyan in 1864.[127] If the opium revenue is to be retained while the monopoly is abolished, there is only one practicable course to be pursued. A Customs duty must be laid on the export of all opium. And this method has obtained the support of many able men who, objecting to the opium traffic as at present conducted, and at the same time seeing the difficulties in the way of its total abolition, propose this compromise. Such are Sir Bartle Frere,[128] Sir Richard Temple, the Marquis of Hartington, and others. But there are many serious drawbacks even to this solution of the difficulty, and such as have always prevailed against it when it has been proposed, as it often has, in Council. On the one hand, the revenue derived from this system would be much less. Sir Evelyn Baring, who is studiously moderate in his figures, informed us in his financial statement for 1882 how much loss would actually in this way ensue. For whereas a chest of Bengal opium costs us to manufacture it 421 Rs., we can sell it for 1,280 Rs. (average of ten years), thus making a clear profit per chest of 859 Rs.; but if we decided to introduce the excise system, the opium would not bear more than 600 Rs. a chest as export duty.[129] The average number of chests exported may be taken as likely to be 45,000. Duty on these would give £2,700,000. But our net revenue from Bengal opium is at least £5,000,000, so that our loss would be nearly two millions and a half; and besides the loss to the Imperial exchequer, the Provincial Governments would lose a part of their income. Moreover, the cost of preventive establishments would be great, and still some part of the produce would evade duty. Again, the cultivators would suffer in every way. Their actual profits would be less, and the zemindars would take the opportunity of squeezing them by rack-renting and other recognized means of oppression, as has been the case in indigo-cultivation, where great disturbances have been caused among the ryots. Add to this that vested interests would be created which would render any return to the old system very difficult, if not impossible. On the other hand—and this must be clear even to the anti-opiumists—India would not release herself from the responsibility of the traffic, whatever that may be, by this means. Direct participation in the manufacture may be more undignified for an Imperial Government than merely a share in the profits; but it cannot affect its moral responsibility. Nor would an ounce less opium enter China because of this measure. "The monopoly," says Sir Henry Pottinger, "has rather tended to check than otherwise the production, as it certainly has the exportation, of the drug."

Dismissing, then, this possibility as one perforce abandoned by the opponents of monopolies, no less than by the opponents of opium, the only other alternative left to us is the total abolition of the growth and manufacture of opium in India. But we are confronted with a difficulty to start with. Do the supporters of this theory mean that the cultivation of opium should be forbidden throughout *all* India? If so, how are we to deal with the native States which cultivate the poppy, and derive a considerable, in some cases a principal, part of their revenue from this source? A previous attempt to interfere with this cultivation occasioned serious disturbances, and almost a civil war. Are we ready to go to that length to enforce our advanced ideas of total abstinence on the independent States of Holkar and Scindia? If they do not mean this, how are we to prevent the cultivators in Malwa taking up the trade abandoned by us, and instead of 45,000 chests, sending 90,000 to China yearly? Again, if the poppy culture be strictly forbidden in *all* India, how are the legitimate wants of the Rajpoots and the Sikhs in the Punjaub, and the inhabitants of Orissa and Assam, to be supplied? Shall we go to China for our opium, thereby getting a more deleterious drug at higher prices, and inducing our subjects to substitute for the comparatively beneficial opium the maddening stimulus of bhang and the poisonous mixtures imported under the name of "French brandies," but composed of such deleterious ingredients as potato spirit and fusel oil? It would, indeed, be a strange finale if the success of this agitation should cause China to export opium into India as she already does into Burmah.

Apart from these contingent possibilities the financial objections to this measure are overwhelming in the opinion of all who are or have been responsible for the financial administration of India. The immediate effect of the cessation of the culture of the poppy would be the disturbance of the cultivation of land amounting to 500,000 acres in British India alone, the readjustment of which would be a difficult and troublesome business. But, of course, the point to be chiefly considered is the immense loss of revenue that must unavoidably ensue. Some, no doubt, of this loss might be made good by the cultivation of other crops on the poppy lands, which comprise some of the best land in the presidency; but how much would thus be recouped is uncertain. In any case it would not amount to a tithe of the loss, and would, moreover, go mostly into the pockets of the zemindars, or middlemen. Again, the present staff employed in the manufacture would have to be pensioned, which would be another item of expense. Practically we may assume, then, that the Indian Exchequer would lose some six millions a year; and this loss would have to be met at once. The importance of this opium revenue to India can scarcely be over-estimated. It is, next to the land tax, the largest item in the revenue. It forms one-seventh of all the revenue of India. It is the most easily collected and the most productive tax ever known. It, and it only, by its marvellous increase, has enabled a series of Chancellors of the Indian Exchequer to tide over the difficulties occasioned by unexpected wars and disastrous famines. It has given the Indian Government the power to carry out innumerable sorely-needed reforms in the administration of justice, in the promotion of education, in the organization of the police and the post-office, in the reduction of the salt tax, and in the furtherance generally of public works; and this will seem no exaggeration when it is stated that in the last twenty years opium has poured into the Indian treasury the colossal revenue of £134,000,000 sterling.

Do away with this revenue and we sacrifice all chance of carrying out these reforms to a successful conclusion, and cripple our whole administration in India. But it behoves us to consider how the deficit *could* be met, if it became necessary. And we may here again remark that it is to the utmost degree unlikely that the British tax-payer will put his hand into his own pocket in order to help India out of her difficulties. Nor, if England *did* offer to meet the deficit, would that be a good precedent to establish. A gift of £20,000,000, which the anti-opiumists speak of, would not nearly cover India's loss. It would cost three times that sum in ten years, *i.e.* if the present rate of revenue be maintained, as there is good reason to suppose that it will.[130] How, then, could the loss be made good?

The expenditure, civil and military, might be curtailed by doing away with the separate establishments of the Bombay and Madras Presidencies and centralizing the whole in Bengal. But this curtailment of the civil expenditure could not bring much relief, as it only amounts to £10,000,000 as it is. A reduction of the military establishments, besides being a danger in the face of Russia's advance towards India, would necessitate a corresponding diminution of the independent native armies, a step which would be unpopular if demanded by our Government. However, this will be necessary if the opium revenue be cut off.

Among other possible expedients for increasing the revenue or lowering the expenditure are a cessation of ordinary, as distinguished from *productive*, public works, such as roads, railways; a reimposition of abandoned taxes like the customs duties, the salt tax (lately partially remitted), the tobacco tax, and the income tax—but there are grave objections to all these; or the land tax could be augmented, as the periods for new settlements came round, and these, perhaps, afford the best prospect of an increase of revenue.

Such are the principal heads under which an increase of revenue might on an emergency be secured. But the increase would not in any case be large; and it must not be forgotten that Sir Evelyn Baring, in his Budget statement for 1882, has given it as his opinion (and who is more able to give an opinion on the subject?) that an *aggregate* increase of taxation is not possible, even reduction in some branches absolutely necessary; *while any essential decrease of expenditure is quite out of the question.* So far from the expenditure showing a tendency to decrease, or even to remain stationary, it has increased last year by a million and a half, this year[131] by three millions and more—under a Liberal Government.

Apart from these direct means for making good the loss of the opium revenue, there is the prospective one of a general increase from reproductive public works, and from a prosperous condition of the country; but it must be borne in mind that this would be greatly lessened and impeded by any increase of taxation.

"*It cannot be too clearly understood,*" says Sir Evelyn Baring (sect. 59), "*that neither by any measure tending to develop the resources of the country, nor by any increase of taxation which is practically within the range of possibility, nor by any reduction of expenditure, could the Government of India in any adequate way at present hope to recoup the loss which would accrue from the suppression of the poppy cultivation in India.*"

On the whole, then, we may conclude with Sir Evelyn Baring that without the revenue which she derives from opium India would be insolvent; that is, her expenditure would be permanently in excess of her income. India is by no means a rich country except in the language of poetry, and her inhabitants are perhaps the poorest in the world, the average income of the ryot being twenty-seven rupees a year! On the other hand, the financial prospects of India are not at present so gloomy as Mr. Fawcett and others would have us believe, but under a succession of able financiers, like Sir John Strachey and Sir Evelyn Baring, a wonderful improvement has been effected; but their efforts would have been crippled and their far-sighted policy paralyzed, if it had not been for the magnificent revenue derived from the sale of opium, which has indeed proved, as it has been called, "the sheet anchor" of Indian finance. And if this revenue *be* badly acquired, there is no question but that it has been splendidly applied; and if the Chinese will have opium, as there is no doubt they will, the superfluity of their wealth cannot be better spent than in the amelioration of the lot of the Indian ryot. This is the very class which would suffer most severely from any increase of taxation, and, as Sir Evelyn Baring says, "to tax India in order to provide a cure—which would almost certainly be ineffectual—for the vices of the Chinese would be wholly unjustifiable." In doing a little right to China, let us beware lest we do a great wrong to India.

As to the effects upon Indian commerce of a large diminution of the opium trade, India would lose her present large profits on a product of which she owns a natural monopoly. She would also be obliged to increase her exports largely, the value of which would consequently be depreciated; except that the Indian tea-trade would be benefited by a disturbance of the China trade. Further, India would be forced to reduce her imports, however necessary these may be. Lastly, there is a prospect of a fall in the rate of exchange, and a further depreciation of silver, which would increase her liabilities and imperil her financial position.

Such, then, are the difficulties which are inseparably connected with any sudden cessation of the opium trade; but it remains for us still to notice one proposal emanating from the supporters of the anti-opium policy, which is remarkable for its naïveté. It recommends that England should demand from China other privileges as an equivalent for the renunciation of a formal right, and as an indemnification of a great loss sustained. This equivalent would no doubt take the shape of commercial concessions, such as the opening up of the interior of China to foreign intercourse, the working of the mines in China, which are numerous and valuable, and the construction and working of railways by English engineers. There is no doubt that China offers a large and virgin field to the commercial activity of England, and the result that followed the opening of ports after our two wars with China are sufficiently remarkable. By the first treaty we gained a trade of £2,000,000; by the second of £3,500,000 annually. In our commercial dealings with the Chinese we have to deal not only with "the obstructive policy of the mandarins, but also the passive and unconscious resistance of a people of stagnant ideas, of very limited enterprise, and possessing only primitive means of inter-communication."[132] For a further development of our commercial intercourse, Medhurst goes on to say, two things are wanting:—1st, access to new markets by having new ports opened and by procuring a right to navigate inland waters, and to improve the means of communication; 2nd, a full and frank acknowledgment by the Chinese at all the ports of the right of foreign goods to be covered and protected from inland dues by transit passes. Some such concessions the anti-opiumists would have us demand; but these benevolent protestors against forcing the Chinese forget that concessions of this kind, wrung from an unwilling people, would be far more galling than any importation of opium, which it is quite clear, even to them, that they need not buy if they do not wish it. Moreover, the important point seems to have been overlooked, that *India* would lose her revenue, while the gain from increased intercourse would be wholly on the side of *England*. As it is, the native community in India can hardly believe that there is not a selfish motive at the bottom of this agitation in England, and, should this last proposal be carried out, we could hardly blame them if they pointed to this as a proof that their suspicions were well founded.

We may here briefly notice[133] Li Hung Chang's latest proposal, that he should farm or purchase the monopoly of all the Indian opium; with the intention, he would no doubt himself say, of getting the control of the trade into his own hands, and limiting the import, just as on a previous occasion, in a communication to the Anglo-Opium Society, he asserted that the only object of the Chinese authorities in taxing opium was in the past, as it would be in the future, the desire to repress the traffic.

Considering, then, the sudden abolition of the opium traffic as practically out of the question, and leaving out of sight the undoubtedly possible, though not likely, gradual cessation of the trade between India and China owing to the competition of the native drug, it only remains for us to propose some practical solution of the difficulty, some less heroic method of removing this rock of offence that has so divided the current of English feeling. If we reject the total suppression theory, there are, as it seems, two alternatives, and two only, left to us. We may on the one hand follow the sensible and statesman-like recommendation of Sir Rutherford Alcock in 1869. With a view to test the sincerity of the Chinese Government, and their power to prohibit the growth of the poppy in their own dominions, that experienced Minister proposed, in a Convention which the Chinese seem disposed to ratify, that they should receive an increased duty on opium imported, "and moreover be allowed to test their power and will to limit or diminish the hitherto unchecked production of opium in their own provinces by an understanding with the Indian Government during a certain period not to extend the production in India; and if the Chinese Government kept faith and showed the power greatly to diminish, and more or less rapidly stop, the culture of the poppy altogether, the Indian Government would then, *pari passu*, consider how far they could further co-operate by diminishing their own area of culture, having time to substitute other crops and industries to take its place."

The effects of this arrangement, if carried out, would be clearly the same as those arising from a gradual cessation of the trade through competition with native opium. The cultivation in India would have time to change without serious injury to the growers of the poppy, and trade would by degrees adapt itself to the altered conditions; but the same results would follow, as in the other case, though not to anything like the same extent. The loss of revenue would still be great, but the general growth of other branches of income would be more likely, if any sudden displacement of industry or capital were avoided. But we can hardly escape the conviction that the Chinese would show themselves as unable or as unwilling to stop the cultivation in China, no less than the import from India, as they have ever been. In fact, the lofty utterance of Taou Kwang notwithstanding, the Chinese authorities are very glad to draw a revenue even from the vices of their people, and they would be very reluctant, not to say quite averse, to sacrifice a revenue now amounting to more than two millions. What they *do* want is to obtain a larger share in the profits arising from the sale of the Indian drug. Let those who believe in the "child-like simplicity"[134] of the Chinese pin their faith to such assertions as that of Li Hung Chang quoted above, that the only aim of the Chinese Government in taxing opium is to limit the import, and that their only object in allowing and even encouraging the native growth is to drive out the foreign drug, and, when they have in this way obtained the command of the market, to suppress the cultivation altogether. This air of injured innocence is remarkably effective with some people; but the exquisite plausibility and adroitness of these and other similar pleas must not blind us to their inherent falsity. Li Hung Chang can no more prevent the Chinese from consuming opium than we can prevent our countrymen from drinking wine and spirits and smoking tobacco by mere legislative enactments, and it would be considered a remarkable method for attaining this desirable end if the distillation of spirits were made as free and unrestrained as the brewing of beer.

Lastly—and this would have the advantage of satisfying the only just plea urged by the "Society,"—we might proclaim to China in unmistakeable terms that she was free to carry out her own fiscal policy as suited her best, with regard to opium as well as all other imports. Not that we are disposed to allow that this is an international *duty*, unless it be an international duty also to free China from *all* the conditions we have forced upon her: unless we are ready, for example, to cede Hongkong, to let the Chinese close their ports if they feel inclined, to give up our missionaries to the tender mercies of Chinese fanaticism, or forbid them to set foot within the Celestial Empire.

The ratification of the Chefoo Convention would be a step in this direction, and may well be tried as a temporary measure, though it is manifestly unfair to say that we are guilty of any breach of faith in regard to this convention.[135]

We have now to consider what would be the result of such a policy to India. China would no doubt take advantage of her freedom, and tax Indian opium as heavily as it would bear, and in this way transfer to herself some of the profits which now go to India; but, on the other hand, she would be unwilling to place a prohibitive tariff upon it, knowing, as she well does, that none the less would it enter China by being smuggled in, and the revenue which should go into the imperial coffers would be paid, as before, to the officials in the shape of bribes. India would certainly not lose *all* its revenue; for a considerable part, one-seventh at least, goes to the Straits Settlements and the neighbouring islands, to the Netherlands of India, to Hongkong for export to the islands of the Pacific, and to California. Moreover, Indian opium has a monopoly value, and is, besides, superior in flavour to all other opium—holds, in fact, that place among the various kinds of the drug which champagne holds among wines. So that, on the whole, this policy, which would strike at the very root of the anti-opium agitation, would not, as it seems, have any very alarming effects upon India.

And now we have done. We have tried to point out the fallacy of the principal arguments urged by the Anti-Opium Society against the traffic, and the injustice and dangers involved in the remedies which they propose. But we have not hesitated to acknowlege it when their objections seemed well-founded. Their opinions, it need not be said, have undergone considerable modification since the days of Earl Shaftesbury's memorial; and it is by no means clear yet what the actual policy advocated by a majority of their supporters is. "Some shout one thing and some another, and the greater part know not wherefore they have been called together." And though we have condemned their measures, we must not be thought to be condemning the men. They, we freely admit, are actuated by the highest and noblest motives of benevolence and philanthropy; but in their sensibility to the sufferings of others, they are apt to disregard the justice due to their own countrymen. If one half of the allegations of the missionaries and their supporters could be accepted as true, and brought home to the intelligence of the nation, there would not be a voice raised for the traffic. The cry would not indeed be "Perish India," but "Perish the opium revenue," at whatever cost to England. The very rejection of these extreme opinions by a large majority of those who, from their position and experience, are best qualified to form a judgment on the question, is in itself a strong argument against their truth; and if not true, how pernicious must be the effect of their dissemination! Here is what an Englishman of ability and experience, for many years resident in Hongkong, says: "I say that the missionaries and the Anti-Opium Society, in the course of their agitation for the abolition of the Indo-Chinese opium trade, are vilifying their countrymen and blackening their country in the eyes of the whole world, so that the foreigner can convict us out of our own mouths, and gibe at us for hypocrisy and turpitude, which we are wholly innocent of, and for crimes we have never committed."

But making every allowance for the loftiness of their motives and the sincerity of their opinions, we must take grievous exception to some of their methods of propagandism. Among the numerous pamphlets and tracts published by the society is one called *Poppies: a Talk with Boys and Girls*, of which the reviewer in the *Friend of China*[136] says himself: "To acknowledge our sins and the sins of our fathers to ourselves, and in the face of the world, is painful and humiliating enough; but to tell our children that England is not the brave, generous, Christian country, foremost of the nations in the cause of liberty and religion all the world over, which we should like them to think her, but, on the contrary, capable of the *meanness, hypocrisy, greed,* and *cruelty* of our treatment of China, is a bitter task." Bitter, indeed! and what if it be wholly unjustifiable? There is no high-minded Englishman but will utterly resent and protest against this poisoning of the minds of our children with delusive and exaggerated statements, and thus prejudicing them on a subject which they are not yet of an age to form a fair judgment about.

As to the meanness, hypocrisy, and the rest, we need not say more than we have already said, but may notice in passing that unlimited abuse of England's foreign policy seems, curiously enough, to be a guarantee with some people of the speaker or writer's having the real interests of England at heart; and a man needs only to stigmatize the national policy with the added acrimony of alliteration as "cruel, cowardly, and criminal,"[137] for him to pass for the purest of patriots.

And now, in conclusion, we are content to leave the issue of this controversy to the judgment of our countrymen, feeling sure that, if justice and right are on the side of the agitators, they will succeed; if not, that the agitation will inevitably die a natural death: ever withal remembering the maxim—

Magna est veritas et prevalebit.

Footnotes:

[1] April 2, 1883.

[2] The insinuations of Mr. Lock in the *Contemporary* are simply beneath contempt.

[3] Soo Sung, a poet of the eleventh century, says the poppy was grown everywhere.

[4] Com. East Indian Finance 1870, Qu. 5865.

[5] *Ibid.*, Qu. 5855.

[6] A.D. 25-220.

[7] In a work on China published 1857.

[8] A fee of one dollar was regularly left by the smugglers with the commander of the vessel, to be called for by the preventive officer.

[9] Don Sinibaldo, however, attributes this removal to the exactions of the Portuguese douanier. See p. 6 of his pamphlet on opium.

[10] Capt. Hall's *Nemesis*, p. 113.

[11] *Nemesis*, p. 115.

[12] See *Opium*, a paper by F. C. Danvers, 1881.

[13] One tael silver was nominally equivalent to 1,000 cash; the silver had now risen to be worth 16,000 cash.

[14] Tang, the Governor of Canton, himself dealt largely in opium. See *Nemesis*, pp. 84, 113.

[15] A guild of Chinese traders at Canton.

[16] Lord Macartney placidly allowed his interpreter to style him "this red-bristled barbarian tribute-bearer."

[17] Don Sinibaldo says (p. 8) that opium not being expressly mentioned, "fait partie des articles non spécifiés, qui sont tenus de payer un droit d'entrée de cinq pour cent"; but surely this is a mistake.

[18] We can well believe with Capt. Hall that "whatever part the question arising out of the opium trade may have afterwards borne in the complication of difficulties, there is little doubt that the first germ of them all was developed at the moment when the general trade with China became free."— *Nemesis*, p. 79.

[19] Sir J. Davis, Dec. 21, 1855.

[20] £650,000.

[21] Mr. Lay, in a memorandum dated April 1844, gave it as his opinion that the difficulty of admitting opium rested only in the thought that it would be a violation of decorum for His Imperial Majesty to legalize a thing once so strongly condemned. He therefore advocated a change of name.

[22] Sir G. Bonham, April 10, 1851.

[23] Tael = 6s. 8d.

[24] The French took part in the expedition in order to obtain satisfaction for the murder of a missionary in 1856, so that in their case it was strictly a missionary war.

[25] New Kwang, Tangchow, Taiwan (Formosa), Swatow, and Kungchow (Hainan).

[26] Mr. Lay, secretary to Lord Elgin's mission.

[27] Lord Elgin had been instructed by Lord Clarendon to ascertain whether the Chinese Government would revoke its prohibitions on opium. "Whether," says Lord Clarendon, "the legalization would tend to augment the trade may be doubtful, as it seems now to be carried to the full extent of the demand in China with the sanction and connivance of the local authorities."

[28] It was currently reported in North China that this officer received 2,000 taels from English merchants for memorializing the Emperor. The edict *did* benefit the foreign trade at first.

[29] Sir Rutherford Alcock, *Nineteenth Century*, Dec. 1881, p. 861.

[30] From sixteen taels at Chinkiang to eighty-four taels at Foochow and Amoy.

[31] Ichang, Wenchow, Wuhu, and Pakhoi.

[32] Sept. 13, 1876.

[33] Dr. Moore, *The Other Side of the Opium Question*, p. 85.

[34] Sir Rutherford Alcock, *Journal of Society of Arts*, p. 220, b.

[35] Dr. Moore (p. 84) quotes Mr. Gardner's opinion to this effect.

[36] *Times*, Jan. 26, 1881. To the same effect is the evidence of Don Sinibaldo, who says (p. 3), "On prétend que l'opium produit chez lui une délicieuse ivresse, un doux sommeil, une vive surexcitation qui deviennent nécessaires á l'existence, et qu'on ne peut obtenir qu'en augmentant progressivement la dose journalière. Pour moi, j'ai souvent fumé de l'opium, et je n'ai éprouvé

rien de semblable; un grand nombre d'Européens qui avaient fait la même épreuve m'ont assuré qu'elle avait eu pour eux les mêmes résultats que pour moi." Perhaps a remark of Dr. Moore (p. 34) may explain these statements. He says, "If the opium-pipe is smoked as the tobacco-pipe is smoked, the effects are very inconsiderable as compared with the results when the novice has attained to perfection in his practice"—*i.e.* can pass the smoke through his lungs.

[37] Colonel Tod, in his book on the Rajpoots, draws a strong picture of the evil effects of opium consumption among them. Of this Sir Henry Lawrence, in a letter to Sir John Kaye, 1854, says, "There is little, if any, truth in it."

[38] Comm. on E. I. Finance, 1871, evidence of Sir Cecil Beadon. Dr. Birdwood, in a letter to the *Times*, Jan. 20, 1882, says: "The Rajpoots, though they are all from youth upward literally saturated with opium, are one of the finest, most truthful, and bravest people in the world. The same may be said of the Sikhs."

[39] *The Other Side of the Opium Question*, pp. 13, 42.

[40] Similarly the Hurkarah, who carries letters and runs messages in India, provided with a small piece of opium, a bag of rice and a lump of bread, will perform incredible journeys.—Sir Rutherford Alcock, Paper before Society of Arts, p. 223.

[41] The extract of hemp drunk as a decoction or swallowed as a drug. See *Report on Excise in the Punjaub*, 1880-1881, sect. 24.

[42] Moore, p. 90.

[43] A sear = 2 lbs.

[44] See Memorandum by Sir Charles Aitchison, *passim*, especially App. to Report, p. 13.

[45] Report by Mr. Weidemann, deputy-commissioner in Henzada, in Parliamentary paper relating to opium in British Burmah, sect. 11.

[46] "British Burmah," an article in the *Times* for Aug. 20, 1882.

[47] See a note appended to Sir Charles Aitchison's Report by Mr. C. Bernard, officiating Chief Commissioner in British Burmah.

[48] *Times*, Aug. 20, 1882.

[49] Memorandum, sect. 9.

[50] *Cf.* the havoc wrought by the "blue flame," introduced by Europeans, among the Red Indians of America.

[51] Memorandum, sect. 4.

[52] Memorandum, sect. 13.

[53] Bringing in a revenue of £175,000.

[54] Dr. Christlieb.

[55] *Confessions of an English Opium-Eater*, p. 5.

[56] Dr. Moore, p. 11, 48, 55.

[57] *Ibid.*, p. 56.

[58] July 12, 1883. This has now been further reduced.

[59] Dr. Christlieb says 1,033,000 acres—an obvious exaggeration.

[60] The districts of Indore, Bhopal, &c.

[61] Mr. Storrs Turner himself, the secretary of the Society, allows that this is a difficult part of the question. See his article in the *Nineteenth Century*, Feb. 1882.

[62] Mr. Brereton (p. 74) estimates the amount consumed in California alone to be worth £100,000.

[63] Mr. Acheson, in a memorandum to the Custom inspectorate from Canton, says it amounts to 5,000 piculs.

[64] This, however, does not fairly represent the difference, as Indian opium yields twenty per cent. more extract.

[65] Brereton, p. 139.

[66] Financial Statement, 1882, sect. 172.

[67] The Right Hon. J. Whittaker Ellis.

[68] Dr. Christlieb, a German professor, says 400,000; but Dr. Medhurst, a medical man resident for years in China, with all his life-long experience and knowledge would not even hazard a conjecture as to the annual death-rate. Dr. Lockhart says, "It is impossible to say what is the number of such victims either among the higher or lower classes." *Ait Varius, negat Scaurus. Utri creditis, Quirites?*

[69] Don Sinibaldo (p. 11). To prohibit opium, he says, because some people kill themselves with it, is as bad as if we prohibited razors because some people cut their throats with them. He also says that he considers the number of deaths by opium in China to be less in proportion than the number of deaths self-inflicted by firearms in France—*i.e.* that they do not number 3,500 in all.

[70] Swinhoe's *Campaign of 1860*, p. 248.

[71] Dr. Ayres, *Friend of China*, 1878, p. 217.

[72] Comm. on E. I. Finance, Q. 5980. Mr. Winchester says: "I should say the balance was in favour of the relief given by the stimulant over the actual misery created by its abuse." Also Dr. Moore, p. 86.

[73] Dr. Ayres, *Friend of China*, 1878, p. 217.

[74] Dr. Myers, *Health of Takow*, p. 8. A recent article in the Times, from a Singapore correspondent, fully bears this out. He says that all allow the Chinese of the Straits Settlements to be the *finest specimens of their race*, and yet these very Chinese, a million in number, smoke 12,000 chests of opium a year; and the deaths from opium registered in the annual medical report were last year *five*.

[75] Mr. Brereton (p. 8) says: "I have known numbers, certainly not less than 500 in all, who have smoked opium from their earliest days, young men, middle-aged, and men of advanced years, some of them probably excessive smokers; but I have never observed any symptoms of decay in one of them." Again: "I have tried to find the victims of the dreadful drug, but have never succeeded."

[76] From a letter to the *London and China Telegraph*, June 19, 1882.

[77] The estimate of one million given in a preceding note includes the Chinese population of the neighbouring islands and of Cochin China.

[78] Dr. Myers: "It is surprising how few among the hard-working class indulge to excess; and case after case will be met with, even in the lowest ranks of life, of men who have smoked regularly from ten to twenty or thirty years, and show little or no signs of mental or physical deterioration."

[79] Dr. Myers, *Health of Takow*, p. 10.

[80] Correspondent to *North China Herald*. See Brereton, p. 135.

[81] Of this the Indian Government is only responsible for 40,000 chests. The rest is Malwa opium.

[82] It may be said that those who smoke *Indian* opium are the richer classes, and therefore more prone to excess; but, on the other hand, the native drug is more deleterious.

[83] *Health of Takow*, p. 6.

[84] *Ibid.*, p. 5.

[85] Mr. Cooper's coolies carried him twenty miles a day for months.

[86] Coleridge.

[87] Aug. 19, 1882.

[88] "Most remarkable for industry and usefulness."—Sir F. Halliday.

[89] See Johnston's *Chemistry of Common Life*.

[90] "Stimulants are weak narcotics: narcotics are strong stimulants."—*Modern Thought*, Aug. 1882.

[91] Sir George Birdwood calls this the greatest temperance triumph of any age or nation.

[92] It has only recently been discovered that the aborigines of Australia also have a narcotic of their own, which has qualities akin to opium and tobacco.

[93] Capt. Hall's *Nemesis*.

[94] *Opium Question Solved*, p. 15. *Cf.* Sir Charles Trevelyan, Comm. on E. I. Finance, Qu. 1532-40.

[95] And in this connection it might occur to us that if, in the wake of our civilization, instead of the "blue ruin" which we gave him, we had brought to the Red Indian the marvellous gift of opium, "that noble race and brave" would not have "passed away," but be still surviving to smoke the calumet of peace with the divine opium in the bowl.

[96] Parliamentary Papers 1842-56, No. 26.

[97] Letter to Sir W. Parker, 1843. He adds that "personally he had not been able to discover a *single* instance of its decidedly bad effects."

[98] *China and the Chinese*.

[99] "No one," says Mr. Gardner, "is maddened by smoking opium to crimes of violence, nor does the habit of smoking increase the criminal returns or swell the number of prison inmates."

[100] Dr. Pereira, *Materia Medica*. Dr. Andrew Clarke estimated on one occasion that seven-tenths of the patients in St. Bartholomew's Hospital owed their ill-health to alcohol.

[101] Dr. Tanner's *Practice of Medicine*. Dr. Moore. For an interesting comparison between opium and alcohol, we may refer our readers to De Quincey's *Confessions of an Opium Eater*.

[102] Twenty-five drops of laudanum = 1 grain of opium ∴ 8,000 drops = 320 grains; but Dr. Myers tells us that 2 grains of opium swallowed = 1 mace (58 grains) smoked, so that De Quincey took what was equivalent to 160 *mace* smoked.

[103] Theodore Gautier maintains that "the love of the ideal is so innate in man that he attempts, as far as he can, to relax the ties which bind body to soul; and as the means of being in an ecstatic state are not in the power of all, one drinks for gaiety, another smokes for forgetfulness, a third devours momentary madness."

[104] It is indeed said of Ennius that he sought inspiration in the flowing bowl; that he never

> "Nisi potus ad arma
> Exsiluit dicenda."—*Hor.*

But then, as Praed says, "poets tell confounded lies," and this may be one of them. Coleridge, in later times, is said to have sought the same inspiration from opium; and poems like "Kubla Khan" testify that he found it.

[105] Enough, as Mr. Brereton says, to form a devil's punchbowl huge enough for all the population of the British Isles to swim in at the same time.

[106] Dr. Norman Kerr in a paper read at the Social Science Congress.

[107] "Any serious attempt to check the evil must originate with the people themselves," said the Chinese Commissioners to Sir Thomas Wade.

[108] To chastise the insolent barbarian, as Lord Palmerston put it to his electors at Tiverton.

[109] A similar proposal to establish a Russian protectorate over the members of the Greek Church in Turkey is thus spoken of by Lord Clarendon: "No sovereign, having a due regard for his own dignity and independence, could admit proposals which conferred upon a foreign and more powerful sovereign a right of protection over his own subjects."

[110] pp. 35-37.

[111] From the latest Parliamentary Paper, containing the correspondence between the Indian and English Governments on the subject of the negotiations with China, it appears (sects. 43-50) that neither the British nor Indian Government has any objection to the ratification of the Chefoo Convention. The *difficulty is to get the other Powers to agree.*

[112] Sir Evelyn Baring. Financial Statement on India for 1882.

[113] A late medical missionary.

[114] Brereton, p. 50. It appears, however, that there are 6,000 Christians already in Japan, the result of fourteen years' preaching.

[115] Intense dislike to foreigners and foreign intercourse was an ever-present reason for condemning a drug which, more than anything else, kept the gates of the empire ajar to the "foreign devils."—*Opium Question Solved.*

[116] Comm. on E. I. Finance 1871, Q. 5831.

[117] The same who has lately been in correspondence with the leaders of the Anti-Opium League.

[118] Comm. on E. I. Finance, Q. 5834.

[119] *Ibid.*, Q. 5817.

[120] *Story of the Fuh-kien Mission*, p. 188.

[121] Capt. Hall, *Nemesis*, p. 375.

[122] *Story of the Fuh-kien Mission*, p. 252.

[123] *Times*, Aug. 22, 1882.

[124] *Times*, Aug. 22, 1882.

[125] *Times*, Aug. 22, 1882.

[126] Brereton, p. 68.

[127] See minute by Sir William Muir, Feb. 1868.

[128] Speech at Newcastle, 1880.

[129] Malwa bears a duty of 650, but the consistence of Malwa chest is 90-95, of Bengal 70-75.

[130] Owing to bad crops the revenue from opium *has* considerably diminished in the last two years, but the present (1884) crop promises exceedingly well.

[131] 1882.

[132] Consul Medhurst, 1872.

[133] Sir Rutherford Alcock's paper before the Society of Arts, p. 225.

[134] Justin McCarthy, *History of Our Own Times*, vol. i., p. 181.

[135] Parliamentary Paper, 1882.

[136] The organ of the Society.

[137] Sir Wilfrid Lawson on the Egyptian War.